OLD TESTAMENT GUIDES

General Editor
R.N. Whybray

JONAH AND LAMENTATIONS

Other titles in this series include

Genesis 1–11
J.W. Rogerson

Genesis 12–50
R.W.L. Moberly

Exodus
W. Johnstone

Leviticus
L.L. Grabbe

Deuteronomy
R.E. Clements

Judges
A.D.H. Mayes

1 & 2 Samuel
R.P. Gordon

1 & 2 Chronicles
G. Jones

Ezra and Nehemiah
H.G.M. Williamson

Job
J.H. Eaton

Psalms
J. Day

Ecclesiastes
R.N. Whybray

The Song of Songs
A. Brenner

Isaiah 56–66
G.I. Emmerson

The Second Isaiah
R.N. Whybray

Jeremiah
R.P. Carroll

Ezekiel
H. McKeating

Daniel
P.R. Davies

Hosea
G.I. Davies

Amos
A.G. Auld

Micah, Nahum, Obadiah
R. Mason

Zephaniah, Habakkuk, Joel
R. Mason

Haggai, Zechariah, Malachi
R.J. Coggins

JONAH & LAMENTATIONS

R.B. Salters

Published by JSOT Press
for the Society for Old Testament Study

For Audrey

אשת חיל

Copyright © 1994 Sheffield Academic Press

Published by JSOT Press
JSOT Press is an imprint of
Sheffield Academic Press Ltd
343 Fulwood Road
Sheffield S10 3BP
England

Typeset by Sheffield Academic Press
and
Printed on acid-free paper in Great Britain
by Charlesworth Group
Huddersfield

A catalogue record for this book is available
from the British Library

ISBN 1-85075-719-4

CONTENTS

Acknowledgments 7
Abbreviations 8

Part I: Jonah

	Select List of Commentaries	13
1.	Introduction	15
2.	Outline of the Book	17
3.	The Place of the Book in the Old Testament	19
4.	The Date of Jonah	23
5.	The Integrity of the Book	28
6.	Genre	41
7.	The Purpose of the Book	51

Part II: Lamentations

	Select List of Commentaries	65
1.	Introduction	67
2.	Outline of the Book	73
3.	Historical Background	76
4.	The Poetry of Lamentations	84
5.	Authorship	93
6.	Genre	101
7.	The Theology of the Book	109

Index of Biblical References 121
Index of Authors 124

ACKNOWLEDGMENTS

I have pleasure in expressing my thanks to: the Department of Old Testament in the University of South Africa for their generosity in inviting me as Visiting Professor, January to March 1989, enabling me to begin work on this book and to try out some of my early thoughts on Jonah; Princeton Theological Seminary for inviting me to spend part of my sabbatical leave there in 1993, and where I finished the work on both parts of this volume; Delbert R. Hillers of the Johns Hopkins University who graciously gave me access to the proofs of the second edition of his commentary on Lamentations; Iain W. Provan of the University of Edinburgh who was good enough to provide me with an advance copy of his commentary on Lamentations.

I am also very grateful to Professor R.N. Whybray for the invitation to write this volume for the Old Testament Guides series, and for his patience, comments, advice and wise counsel at various stages of its creation. Gregory P. Morris, currently a doctoral student at the University of St Andrews, assisted me with the indexing and proofreading. Finally, for her support and encouragement, I wish to thank my wife, Audrey, to whom this volume is dedicated, and to whom I owe so much.

Robert B. Salters
University of St Andrews
December 1993

ABBREVIATIONS

AB	Anchor Bible
AJT	*American Journal of Theology*
AnBib	Analecta Biblica
ANET	J.B. Pritchard (ed.), *Ancient Near Eastern Texts*
ATD	Das Alte Testament Deutsch
Bib	*Biblica*
BHK	R. Kittel (ed.), *Biblica hebraica*
BHS	*Biblia hebraica stuttgartensia*
BKAT	Biblischer Kommentar: Altes Testament
BSac	*Bibliotheca Sacra*
BZ	*Biblische Zeitschrift*
BZAW	Beihefte zur ZAW
CBQ	*Catholic Biblical Quarterly*
CBS	Cambridge Bible for Schools
CNEB	Commentary on the New English Bible, Cambridge
CTJ	*Calvin Theological Journal*
DSB	Daily Study Bible
EncJud	*Encyclopaedia Judaica*
ExpTim	*Expository Times*
HDB	J. Hastings (ed.), *A Dictionary of the Bible*
HTR	*Harvard Theological Review*
HUCA	*Hebrew Union College Annual*
IB	Interpreter's Bible
ICC	International Critical Commentary
IDB	G.A. Buttrick (ed.), *Interpreter's Dictionary of the Bible*
IDBSup	*IDB*, Supplementary Volume
IEJ	*Israel Exploration Journal*
Int	*Interpretation*
ITC	International Theological Commentary
JB	Jerusalem Bible
JBL	*Journal of Biblical Literature*
JJS	*Journal of Jewish Studies*
JNES	*Journal of Near Eastern Studies*
JPOS	*Journal of the Palestine Oriental Society*
JQR	*Jewish Quarterly Review*
JSOT	*Journal for the Study of the Old Testament*
JSOTSup	*JSOT* Supplement Series

Abbreviations

KAT	Kommentar zum Alten Testament
MLB	Modern Language Bible: New Berkeley Version
NCB	New Century Bible
NEB	New English Bible
NICOT	New International Commentary on the Old Testament
NJV	New Jewish Version (Jewish Publication Society)
OS	Oudtestamantische Studiën
OTE	Old Testament Essays
OTL	Old Testament Library
OuTWP	Die Ou Testamentiese Werkgemeenskap Suid-Afrika
PTR	Princeton Theological Review
RB	Revue biblique
REB	Revised English Bible
RHPR	Revue d'historie et de philosophie religieuses
RSV	Revised Standard Version
SBT	Studies in Biblical Theology
SJOT	Scandinavian Journal of the Old Testament
TynBul	Tyndale Bulletin
VT	Vetus Testamentum
VTSup	Vetus Testamentum, Supplements
ZAW	Zeitschrift für die alttestamentliche Wissenschaft
ZDMG	Zeitschrift der deutschen morgenländischen Gesellschaft

Part I

JONAH

Select List of Commentaries

L.C. Allen, *The Books of Joel, Obadiah, Jonah and Micah* (NICOT; London: Hodder & Stoughton, 1976). This is a carefully and lucidly written commentary, short enough not to swamp the beginner but of sufficient length and depth to take its place along with the main commentaries.

J.A. Bewer, *A Critical and Exegetical Commentary on Haggai, Zechariah, Malachi and Jonah* (ICC; Edinburgh: T. & T. Clark, 1912). While this is rather dated now, it remains a useful commentary. Students with a knowledge of Hebrew will get most from it.

L.H. Brockington, 'Jonah', in M. Black and H.H. Rowley (eds.), *Peake's Commentary on the Bible* (London: Nelson, 1962), pp. 627-29. This is a very short work which may serve as a first commentary for the student.

F.W. Golka, *The Song of Songs and Jonah* (Edinburgh: Handsel Press; Grand Rapids: Eerdmans, 1988). This is a short commentary in a series which attempts to go beyond the descriptive–historical approach 'to offer a relevant exegesis of the Old Testament as Holy Scripture'.

J. Magonet, *Form and Meaning: Studies in Literary Techniques in the Book of Jonah* (Sheffield: Almond Press, 1983). This is not quite a commentary as such, but it is a very thorough treatment of the book. The author is inclined to disregard critical scholarship and imagines a very complex structure to the book. Again, Hebrew is needed for a full appreciation.

J.M. Sasson, *Jonah—A New Translation with Introduction, Commentary, and Interpretation* (AB: Garden City, NY: Doubleday, 1990). The most recent and the most comprehensive commentary: 368 pages full of information and detail, not only on Jonah but on related literature.

J.D. Smart, 'Jonah', *IB*, VI (Nashville: Abingdon Press, 1956). This is a well-written commentary in a series found in most libraries.

P.L. Trible, 'Studies in the Book of Jonah' (PhD dissertation, Columbia University, 1963). This is not a verse-by-verse commentary but it is well worth consulting on many matters.

G.W. Wade, *Micah, Obadiah, Joel and Jonah* (London: Methuen, 1925). Although dated, this commentary offers the student a good introduction and a great deal of information.

J.D.W. Watts, *The Books of Joel, Obadiah, Jonah, Nahum, Habakkuk* (Cambridge: Cambridge University Press, 1975). Although quite a short commentary it will serve the beginner well.

H.W. Wolff, *Obadiah and Jonah* (Minneapolis: Augsburg; London: SPCK, 1986). Easily the best commentary in English (translated from the German). Although a knowledge of Hebrew is necessary to understand fully the author's arguments, the non-Hebraist will benefit greatly. There is a very full and useful bibliography.

Foreign-language commentaries

F.W. Golka, *Jona* (Calwer Bibelkommentare; Stuttgart: Calwer Verlag, 1991). This is an expanded version of the author's short commentary in English. While a knowledge of Hebrew is useful, it is not essential.

W. Rudolph, *Jona* (KAT, 2; Gütersloh: Gerd Mohn, 1971). This is one of the better commentaries: succinct, and with a good bibliography.

A. Weiser, *Jona* (ATD, 5: Göttingen: Vandenhoeck & Ruprecht, 1967). Short but scholarly.

1

INTRODUCTION

IT IS REMARKABLE how well known the story of Jonah was in antiquity and how popular it has been over the centuries down to the present day. We should expect it to be alluded to in Jewish literature such as rabbinic writings, and this is the case: there are many such references. Again, we find it referred to in the New Testament in Mt. 12.40 and Lk. 11.29-32. This latter fact may account for the attention the book has received in Christian writings over the years. In the Koran, too, Jonah is mentioned, and in Islamic legend he is a favourite subject.

It is, perhaps, not surprising that writers within Judaism, Christianity and Islam should allude to the book, for it is, after all, part of Scripture. What *is* surprising is the extent of the book's popularity even in circles on the outskirts of these movements. Somehow the story has inspired writers, musicians and artists. Jonah is particularly well attested in art. There are, for example, many instances of the story represented in the Roman catacombs and on sarcophagi from the early centuries of this era, the themes being the storm at sea, the swallowing and the regurgitation of Jonah and the disagreement which he has with God. In the Sistine Chapel and Santa Maria del Popolo in Rome are to be found representations of the prophet by Michelangelo and Raphael. Byzantine manuscripts reveal that Jonah was a popular figure during that period. Later, Rubens and Poussin painted pictures of Jonah which show that he continued to fascinate the human mind.

But it is not only in art that Jonah has been popular. In literature too he appears from mediaeval times to the present century: in 1921 A.P. Herbert wrote a comic dramatization of the story; and Aldous Huxley wrote a poem 'Jonah' in 1959. And in music he has not been omitted: he is the subject of a seventeenth-century oratorio and, more recently, his name is the title of another by Lennox Berkeley. Why this popularity? Part of the reason must lie in the fact that the book is a story, and a story is more easily remembered than a prophetic oracle, a set of laws or a genealogy. Thus the stories of Joseph, Moses, Abraham and David are all subjects treated in the arts in general. But part of the reason has to do with the unusual episode of the fish. It is the swallowing and vomiting of Jonah which have caught the imagination in much the same way that Daniel in the lions' den, Elijah and the prophets of Baal or Noah and the ark have done. While other aspects of the story are depicted in the arts, the main incident portrayed is that of Jonah in (and out of) the belly of the fish. The fact that Mohammed refers to no other Hebrew prophet but Jonah and alludes to him as 'the man of the fish' underlines this point.

Further Reading

G.H. Cohn, 'Jonah', *EncJud*, X, pp. 169-77.
Wolff, *Obadiah and Jonah*, pp. 92-93.

See also
S. Andres, *Der Mann im Fisch* (Munich: R. Piper, 1963).
L. Berkeley, *Jonah* (London: J. & W. Chester, 1935).
A. Camus, *The Exile and the Kingdom* (New York: Knopf, 1957).
A.P. Herbert, *The Book of Jonah* (1921).
L. Housman, 'The Burden of Nineveh', in *Old Testament Plays* (London: Cape, 1950).
A. Huxley, 'Jonah', in *Verses and a Comedy* (London: Chatto & Windus, 1946).

2
OUTLINE OF THE BOOK

JONAH IS ONE OF THE shortest books among the Twelve Prophets, consisting of four short chapters, three of which are in narrative form. The chapter division in the Hebrew Bible differs slightly from that in the English in that ch. 2 of the Hebrew begins with 'And the Lord appointed a great fish', that is, at 1.17 in the English.

1.1-3: God's Challenge to Jonah

God commissions Jonah, who does not reply but makes plans which preclude obedience.

1.4-16: Scene at Sea

God causes a violent storm, and disaster looms; the sailors pray while Jonah sleeps. The captain accuses Jonah of apathy (1.4-6). The sailors suspect that someone on board has angered a god; they cast lots, and Jonah is singled out; he confesses and suggests they throw him overboard (1.7-12).

The sailors try to row ashore, but in vain, and reluctantly throw Jonah overboard. The storm ceases, and the sailors sacrifice to God and make vows (1.13-16).

1.17–2.10: Jonah is Miraculously Saved

God causes a fish to swallow Jonah, and he remains in the belly of the fish for three days and three nights; he prays to God (1.17–2.1).

2.2-9 consists of a prayer of thanksgiving by Jonah in psalm form. In v. 10 God causes the fish to regurgitate Jonah onto dry land.

3.1-10: Jonah's Successful Mission to Nineveh

Jonah preaches in Nineveh, and the people repent (3.1-5). The king of Nineveh proclaims a fast and repentance (3.6-9). God changes his plan to destroy Nineveh (3.10).

4.1-11: Jonah's Dispute with God

Jonah is angry with events and wants to die (4.1-5). God causes first a plant to grow up in order to shade Jonah from the sun, then a worm to attack the plant, and a sultry wind to sap Jonah's energy. Jonah again wants to die; and God argues from Jonah's experience that the Ninevites should be spared (4.6-11).

3
THE PLACE OF THE BOOK IN THE OLD TESTAMENT

Affinities

NEARLY EVERY COMMENTARY on the book draws attention to the fact that Jonah is unique, and quite different from the other prophetic books in the Old Testament because of the nature of its composition and form; and it does seem likely that had this book not included the name Jonah ben Amittai, or had omitted the phrase 'ben Amittai', it might well not have appeared among the prophets in the Hebrew Bible. Having said that, it must be stressed that the book does have strong links with other Old Testament literature.

Quite apart from the fact that the book is written in classical Hebrew, its narrative in the style of other Old Testament narratives and its poetry like that of Psalms, there are phrases and touches which anchor it firmly in the Old Testament. It begins in a similar way to Hosea, Joel, Micah and Zephaniah. The command by Yahweh to Jonah is reminiscent, in form at least, of other commands by Yahweh to Amos (7.15), Jeremiah (18.1) and Hosea (1.2), for example. The customs of casting lots, sacrificing, making vows, praying, proclaiming a fast, wearing sackcloth, sitting in ashes, and the royal decree all find echoes in other parts of the Old Testament; and Jonah's confession in 4.2 betrays a connection with Joel 2.13 and Exod. 34.6 (cf. Nah. 1.3; Ps. 103.8).

Again, when mention is made of place-names, such as Joppa, Nineveh and Tarshish, these are all familiar to the reader of the Old Testament (see for example Ezra 3.7; Gen. 10.11; Isa. 23.1); and the name Jonah ben Amittai is actually mentioned in 2 Kgs 14.25. Furthermore, when beasts are included in the decree of the King of Nineveh (3.7-9), we are reminded of the commandment regarding the Sabbath (Exod. 20.10), the cattle looking up to God in Joel (1.20) and the linking of 'man and beast' in punishment in Jeremiah (7.20).

Attention is sometimes drawn to other, less precise similarities. For example, Jonah's flight is thought to echo Elijah's flight in 1 Kings 17–19, although the reasons are quite different. Both men are dejected and both request death (1 Kgs 19.4; Jon. 4.3); and, it is claimed, the juniper tree is paralleled by the castor oil plant (1 Kgs 19.4; cf. Jon. 4.6). In the Elijah story God pleads twice with Elijah, and there is a similar repetition in Jonah, first in the repeated call (1.2; 3.2-3), and then in the double question regarding Jonah's anger (4.4; 4.9). Furthermore, some see in the story shades of Ezek. 27.25-27, which speaks of the sinking of the ships of Tarshish.

Finally, the theology assumed by the author is not unfamiliar. The creation theology of Genesis 1 and Deutero-Isaiah is quite clearly visible in 1.9 and in the various references to God's being in control of the wind and the sea (cf. also the exodus and flood stories), the fish, the plant and the worm. The view that expects sin to be punished is also clearly drawn, both in the scene at sea and in the concern expressed by God regarding the evil of Nineveh. The fact that God is approachable and may change his mind is also familiar (Jer. 18.7-8); and if we were to compare the psalm of ch. 2 with the book of Psalms, we might find as many as 22 quotations or imitations in vv. 3-10. Hence in only 48 verses, which is the extent of the book, there are so many connections with the Old Testament that one might begin to doubt if Jonah has anything new to say.

Differences

There are, of course, differences. In the structure of the Hebrew Bible—Law, Prophets, Writings—Jonah stands out among the Prophets generally, and in the subdivision known as the Minor Prophets in particular, as being a very different kind of literature. For the most part the books of the prophets

3. The Place of the Book in the Old Testament

in the Old Testament comprise collections of prophetic sayings or oracles, with an occasional story about a particular prophet. The book of Jonah is not like this; it is, rather, a story about a prophet, and contains only one very brief oracle (3.4). That is perhaps the most striking difference. The reader is, however, also occasionally surprised at events, phrases and situations. For example, Jonah's disobedience comes as a bolt out of the blue; one expects (from one's reading elsewhere in Scripture) the command to be followed by obedience. The incident in which Jonah is swallowed by the fish is, again, unparalleled in the Old Testament, while the composing of a psalm in the fish's belly is quite astonishing. Not quite so astonishing are the passages which refer to God speaking to the fish and appointing the fish, the plant, the worm and the wind; but they do tend to distance the book from other parts of the Old Testament. Again, we have no other reference in the Old Testament to a king of Nineveh, nor is there a parallel to the phenomenon of whole cities repenting. Finally, it is somewhat surprising to find in a prophetic book no mention of Yahweh's covenant with Israel.

Jonah and the Canon

In the Hebrew Bible the book of Jonah is found in the section known as 'the Book of the Twelve Prophets' (sometimes called 'the Minor Prophets'). In the Apocrypha, in the book of Ecclesiasticus, mention is made of the twelve prophets (49.10). As the writer has just referred to Isaiah, Jeremiah and Ezekiel, it is likely that the reference is to the twelve short books, Hosea to Malachi, reckoned as one book in the Jewish canon.

In this section Jonah stands fifth, after Hosea, Joel, Amos and Obadiah. It is not certain what determined this order, but it is likely that the compilers felt that, as in the case of the order of Isaiah, Jeremiah and Ezekiel, they were placing the books in chronological sequence. The reference to Jonah ben Amittai (1.1) would remind them of the passage in 2 Kgs 14.23-25 where a prophet of that name appears and where the historical context is that of the reign of Jeroboam II. This might account for the book's appearance after Amos and before Micah. Its position after Obadiah is more problematic, but may be explained by assuming that the editors identified the Obadiah of 1.1 with the Obadiah who appears in the time of Ahab (1 Kgs 18.3-5); that is to say, although the compilers may not always have been correct in their judgments, their criterion may have been chronological.

In the Septuagint the book of Jonah is followed by that of Nahum. This suggests different considerations at work. Since the compilers of the Greek version had a different literary approach to the various groupings, it may be that they noticed that both books deal with Nineveh, albeit rather differently; also both allude to the covenant statement of Exod. 34.6 (Nah. 1.2-3a; cf. Jon. 4.2) and each ends with a question.

Further Reading

For the most up-to-date discussion on these matters see Sasson, *Jonah*, pp. 13-15.

See also D.A. Schneider, 'The Unity of the Book of the Twelve' (PhD dissertation, Yale University, 1979).

4
THE DATE OF JONAH

ALTHOUGH IT USED TO BE taken for granted that the book was written in the eighth century BCE by Jonah ben Amittai, the book itself does not so claim; indeed, it is not written in the first person but in the third. In fact, scholars nowadays have abandoned the pre-exilic date for the composition in favour of a post-exilic date.

Since the book begins with a reference to Jonah ben Amittai the *terminus a quo* must surely be in the reign of Jeroboam II of Israel whose dates are c. 786–746 BCE. The text of 2 Kings reads:

> In the fifteenth year of Amaziah the son of Joash, king of Judah, Jeroboam the son of Joash, king of Israel, began to reign in Israel, and he reigned forty-one years. And he did what was evil in the sight of the Lord; he did not depart from all the sins of Jeroboam the son of Nebat, which he made Israel to sin. He restored the border of Israel from the entrance of Hamath as far as the Sea of the Arabah, according to the word of the Lord, the God of Israel, which he spoke by his servant Jonah the son of Amittai, the prophet, who was from Gath-hepher (2 Kgs 14.23-25).

On the question of date some information may be deduced from the reference in Ecclus 49.10. Since 'the twelve prophets' receives mention there, and since Ecclesiasticus was probably written at the end of the third century BCE, the book cannot have been written after that time; and, since Ecclesiasticus speaks of the twelve reverentially, we may assume that the collection was already canonical, and that the book had been in existence for some time.

Language

Although, as has been observed above, the book of Jonah has affinities with the rest of the Old Testament in terms of language, both prose and poetry, there are some differences which, for some scholars, point to a late date for the composition of the book. These features are not always observable in English.

First of all there are words or phrases which are significant and striking. These fall into two categories: first, those which occur elsewhere in the Old Testament only in late books such as Chronicles, Daniel and Ecclesiastes. For example, the word for 'sailor' (1.5-6) occurs only in Ezek. 27.8-9, 27-29. Then there is the form of the relative pronoun found in 1.7, 12; 4.10; this is found elsewhere only in the late works of Song of Songs (cf. 1.7) and Ecclesiastes (cf. 1.3). Again, the phrase 'the God of heaven' (1.9), although occurring in Gen. 24.3, 7, appears otherwise to be confined to post-exilic literature (2 Chron. 36.23; Ezra 1.2, 5; 2.4, 20; cf. Ps. 136.23). Indeed, the phrase is to be found mostly in the Aramaic portions of the Old Testament and in the Aramaic Elephantine papyri of the fifth century BCE. Since Aramaic was the lingua franca of the Persian Empire it is thought that the phrase originated in that period and passed into Hebrew.

Secondly, there are words which in Old Testament Hebrew occur only in Jonah but which are to be found in Aramaic (late biblical and extrabiblical); for example, 'ship' (1.5), 'to think' (1.6), 'taste' (3.7), 'message' (3.2), 'sultry' (4.8). While it is acknowledged that a solitary appearance of such a word does not necessarily mean that the passage in which it occurs is late—the context or scene being described may be unique and require unusual vocabulary—yet the use of particular expressions such as the 'God of heaven' or the aforementioned relative pronoun point clearly to the post-exilic period.

The Standpoint of the Author

Another factor which may be raised in connection with date is that the author seems to be distant from the pre-exilic period

4. The Date of Jonah

and out of touch with historical reality. The author speaks of the King of Nineveh, thereby implying a city-state; but in the days of Jonah ben Amittai, that is, in the eighth century BCE, there would not have been a king of Nineveh but a king of Assyria, and he would not have resided in Nineveh but in Nimrud. There seems, therefore, to be an anomaly here, for Nineveh is unlikely to have been a city-state at any time in its history, which ended in 612 BCE. Furthermore, the king is never mentioned by name in the text of Jonah (nor is there any mention of a king of Nineveh in Assyrian annals) and so is left unconnected to history.

Again, the description of Nineveh as a great city which took three days to cross is out of touch with reality, since this would imply about forty miles in width, which is quite out of the question; Nineveh of Sennacherib's time was no more than three miles wide. Clearly, this is an exaggeration; and the author is able to express this view because he is writing at a time when no one is able to gainsay him.

In addition, while the place-names mentioned are familiar from other parts of the Old Testament, a close examination of the passages in which they occur reveals that they are not used here in a realistic manner. For example, according to 2 Kgs 14.25 Jonah was from Gath-hepher in Galilee. While this is not mentioned in the book of Jonah we may assume that it was known to the author, and yet he depicts Jonah as going to Joppa to catch a ship. This is strange. Joppa probably did not belong to Israel in the eighth century, nor was it the nearest port to Gath-hepher. This lack of accuracy suggests that the author may have lived in Judah (where Joppa would have had maritime significance), and at a time sufficiently late for Nineveh to have become legendary in size and evil.

Literary Considerations

From a literary point of view there is the argument that Jonah shows a dependence on other parts of the Old Testament, thereby pointing to a late date. It is sometimes claimed that passages such as 1 Kgs 19.4-5; Jer. 1.8, 11; 26.3, 15; Ezek. 27.8, 9, 25-29; 34.6; Joel 1.13; 2.13-14 were all known to our author, and this would mean that he postdated the latest of these. This argument is a difficult one to control, for similarities, such as have been observed, may point in a number of directions. Which is the earlier passage? How can we be sure? Is there a dependence, or do both passages depend on a third passage?

The argument for dependence on Joel is crucial here. A comparison of Joel 2.13-14 with Jon. 3.9 and 4.2 shows a literary relationship:

> Rend your hearts and not your garments. Return to the Lord, your God, for he is gracious and merciful, slow to anger, and abounding in steadfast love, and repents of evil. Who knows whether he will not turn and repent...? (Joel 2.13-14).
>
> Who knows? God may yet repent and turn from his fierce anger, so that we perish not (Jon. 3.9).
>
> I knew that thou art a gracious God and merciful, slow to anger, and abounding in steadfast love, and repentest of evil (Jon. 4.2).

Although there are echoes of Jon. 4.2 in other parts of the Old Testament—for example Exod. 34.6; Neh. 9.17; Ps. 86.15—the passage in Joel is the only other passage which speaks of God repenting of evil. Furthermore, whereas Joel speaks of God repenting towards Israel, Jonah applies this notion to Nineveh, and scholars feel that the latter is derived from the former. It is much more likely that Jonah is using Joel than that Joel is echoing Jonah, for Joel knows nothing of the doctrine with regard to the Gentiles. Since Joel may be dated between 400 and 350 BCE we should allow ourselves to settle for a date for Jonah no earlier than c. 350 BCE. This latter point also agrees with the evidence from vocabulary; but we cannot be more precise.

Further Reading

Allen, *The Books of Joel, Obadiah, Jonah and Micah*, pp. 185-91.
J.J. Glück, 'A Linguistic Criterion of the Book of Jonah', *OuTWP* 1967 (1971), pp. 34-41.
Golka, *Jona*, pp. 44-46.

4. The Date of Jonah

A. Van Selms, 'Some Geographical Remarks on Jonah', *OuTWP* 1967 (1971), pp. 83-92.

R.D. Wilson, 'The Authenticity of Jonah', *PTR* 16 (1918), pp. 280-98, 430-56.

Wolff, *Obadiah and Jonah*, pp. 76-78.

5
THE INTEGRITY OF THE BOOK

VARIOUS INFLUENCES IN present-day biblical studies have tended to turn scholars' attention away from questions of the composition of the books of the Old Testament. The great efforts of scholars in the nineteenth century and early twentieth centuries probably took things to extremes in finding multiple authors for almost every book in the Hebrew Bible. At the end of the last century Siegfried found seven authors involved in the production of Ecclesiastes! And yet it would be a strange scholar who would deny that there were several strata in some books, and that Old Testament books did not come into being in the same way that books do today. Gunkel drew attention also to the growth not only of whole books but of episodes within the literature.

When we come to the book of Jonah, the subject of its composition is one that is not now in fashion, for it calls in question, to some extent, some of the current approaches to the text. One constantly reads phrases like 'a superb piece of literature', 'a masterpiece of storytelling', 'a work of art', 'one of the sublimest creations of the religion of Israel'; and yet when one reads the book one gets the feeling that these are oversimplifications, and that blind eyes are being turned on this book. My point is this: quite apart from the presence in the book of the psalm, which I think is for various reasons difficult to accept as original to the book, and which some of the scholars who sing the praise of the author are inclined to bypass in their assessments, there are problems in the story

5. *The Integrity of the Book* 29

itself which are not easily or satisfactorily explained, and which raise the question of integrity.
Chapter 1 (apart from the phrase in v. 8 'on whose account this evil has come upon us', which appears to be a gloss on a similar phrase in v. 7) seems to me to present no problems of this kind. But—leaving aside ch. 2 for the moment—in ch. 3 problems raise their head. One can be too critical of this type of literature, and I do not wish to query the description of the size of the city of Nineveh (three days across); that is the kind of detail which may be characteristic of this type of story. If this description was not true of Nineveh, as historians and archaeologists tell us, what matter? It may be seen as part of the exaggeration of the story-teller. As Wolff says, 'The reader is not meant to do arithmetic. He is meant to be lost in astonishment'. That may be so. What is surprising is the announcement by Jonah after entering the city: 'In forty days Nineveh shall be overthrown'. The story had moved quite rapidly up to this point—that is part of the skill of the author—but now we are expected to slow down and wait. However, that puzzlement seems to dissolve when we read the Septuagint, which says 'in *three* days...' That seems to fit in better with the pace of the narrative. It is true that the MT is supported by other Greek versions (Aquila, Symmachus, Theodotion) and by the Targum, and it has been argued that the Septuagint reading may be accounted for as an imitation of the number three mentioned in 2.1 and 3.3. But I would follow the Septuagint, and understand the number 40 to reflect a later reading based perhaps on other occurrences of the same number in the Old Testament; for example, Deut. 9.18 which also has to do with penance and repentance. Repentance is admittedly not specifically mentioned in the Jonah passage but v. 5 may constitute an exegesis of Jonah's announcement of doom in terms of repentance (cf. Bewer).

The position of 4.5 has been the subject of much critical discussion. It is not popular nowadays to question it; but several scholars continue to maintain that it properly belongs after 3.4, that is, immediately after the announcement of doom, where they consider it to be more appropriate, and where it serves to keep the story moving. Kraeling, however, argued that 3.5, in which the people of Nineveh repent, was originally followed by 3.10 and that a later writer added the incident about the decree in vv. 7-9.

Again, do we not have to admit that there is something awkward with the passage 4.6-11? No commentator deals satisfactorily with the juxtaposition of the booth and the plant. Furthermore, God's final speech accuses Jonah of pitying the plant when it seems to the reader that Jonah, while welcoming the shade afforded by the plant, is still angry about God's decision to forgive, and that it is this combined with the discomfort of the heat and wind, which has made him ask for death. (The fact that v. 6 begins with the combination 'Lord God' and that 'God' and 'Lord' are both used here may be related to the problem, although no satisfactory rationale of the use of the terms for God here seems to be emerging.)

Finally, it has been suggested that the passage 4.6-10 is secondary, and that v. 4 was originally followed by 'and he said: "I do well to be angry, angry enough to die"' followed by: 'And the Lord said, "Should I not pity Nineveh...cattle?"'

Although some at least of these problems are not insoluble, there are others which need to be tackled.

The Psalm

First and foremost in any discussion of the integrity of the book is the disputed question of the psalm of Jonah in 2.3-10 (ET 2.2-9). Since the advent of literary criticism of the Old Testament there have been scholars who have expressed doubts as to the authenticity of this piece. De Wette was the first to argue that it is a later addition. While there have been recent moves to defend the psalm's authenticity, many scholars remain in the De Wette camp. Some of the latter, while admitting that the psalm was not composed by the prose author, argue that it was taken by him from a cultic context and inserted in his book; others attribute the insertion to a later editor or redactor (see below).

The study of the text of the psalm led to the observation that it is remarkably similar to those in the book of Psalms.

5. The Integrity of the Book

There are so many similarities that it might even have been 'composed' by borrowing phrases and vocabulary from other psalms. Examples are as follows:

2.3a (ET 2a)	cf. Pss. 120.1; 18.7 (ET 6)
2.4b (ET 3b)	cf. Ps. 42.8b (ET 7b)
2.5a (ET 4a)	cf. Ps. 31.23 (ET 22)
2.6a (ET 5a)	cf. Ps. 18.5 (ET 4)
2.7 (ET 6)	cf. Pss. 30.4 (ET 3); 31.20
2.8a (ET 7a)	cf. Pss. 142.4 (ET 3); 143.4
2.9a (ET 8a)	cf. Ps. 31.7 (ET 6)
2.10 (ET 9a)	cf. Ps. 42.5 (ET 4)

The suspicion that the psalm may not be original was not simply based on the fact that it is poetry while the rest of the book is prose, although that argument was also used. Other Old Testament studies had shown that poetry found in the midst of prose might have originally had an independent existence; for example, the prayer of Hezekiah (Isa. 38.10-20) which is lacking in the parallel passage in 2 Kings 20. It was also argued that the psalm in Jonah hardly fits the context. Even before the Old Testament literary critics became active, biblical scholars indicated that they would have expected a prayer of confession and repentance to follow the swallowing of Jonah, not one of praise and thanksgiving. Indeed, Philo of Alexandria, in a retelling of the story in Greek, replaces the psalm with a plea by Jonah for deliverance, while Josephus and Tyndale accept the interpretation that the psalm was uttered *after* Jonah found himself on terra firma. A mediaeval paraphrase of the story also depicts Jonah as praying for restoration. It was instinctively felt that repentance or supplication, and not thanksgiving, should appear here.

The usual explanation for Jonah's not repenting of his initial disobedience is that he was grateful for having escaped drowning, and that the psalm is therefore an appropriate response to his situation. While this interpretation is still adhered to in some circles (especially where the integrity of the text is defended at all costs) it is more usual to find unease among commentators at this point. Josephus's interpretation has led to the suggestion that the psalm has been misplaced and should stand at the end of ch. 2, when Jonah could be certain that he had been delivered. When Day argues that in the belly of the fish it was a case of 'out of the frying pan into the fire' he is expressing the natural and general response to this passage; and it is crediting Jonah too much by way of faith to suppose that he was aware that the darkness and discomfort of the belly of the fish was the first stage in an ultimate deliverance; besides, even if Jonah were capable of such faith, we should still expect thanks to be preceded by remorse for disobedience.

Again, it is argued, when we examine the scenes in which Jonah appears in the rest of the book we find a character who is rebellious, given to self-pity, despairing; indeed, in the prose of the book Jonah can hardly be said to be depicted other than negatively. The psalm, then, with its devotion and praise to God, seems incongruous, presenting by implication a very different Jonah. It is not an adequate answer to argue that this is in keeping with Jonah elsewhere in that he is always acting clumsily and inconsistently. This divides the psalm's defenders into two camps: those who say that it is natural to thank God while in the fish, and those who say that it is unnatural, but that is what we expect from Jonah!

Furthermore, we might deduce from the prose section that Jonah would rather die than carry out his commission; he even asks the ship's crew to throw him overboard, presumably thinking that this was the end of it all. It is, therefore, odd to find him praising God for his deliverance.

In addition, some point out as an inconsistency that while idolatry is condemned in the psalm (2.9, ET 2.8), in the prose chapters the sailors and the Ninevites, who are pagans, are given a very sympathetic treatment; indeed, it should be noted that the Ninevites are not asked to abandon the worship of other gods, and that there is no evidence that the sailors forsake their worship.

Another point that is sometimes made is that the psalm displays language and vocabulary which are not found in the prose part of the book. Although arguments on grounds of vocabulary, especially when comparing prose with poetry, should never be taken too far, it is interesting that the word 'great' which appears in the prose narrative often (it is almost

5. The Integrity of the Book

a favourite word of the author) is absent from the psalm. Some scholars make other similar observations about points which are not observable in the English translation and which should not be pressed in a comparison of prose with poetry. Wolff, however, makes an interesting and telling point when comparing the psalm with the other prayers in the book, that is 1.14 and 4.2-3. These other prayers actually address God; they do not talk *about* him. They fit in precisely with the prose story, picking up from the context (cf. 1.14 with 1.16; 4.2 with 1.3 and 3.9-10); and they have the same sort of prose form as the context (see also Trible).

There remain a few scholars who are unwilling to surrender the position that the psalm is an integral part of the book, although they are not unanimous in the stance they take. Some argue that the psalm is the work of the prose writer, while others see the psalm as having had an independent existence but as having been chosen and used by the author of the prose. The view that the psalm is the work of the author of the prose chapters is represented by Magonet, who takes up the points raised against the authenticity of the psalm and counters them strongly. He draws attention to words which appear in both psalm and prose, for example the verb 'to go down' which appears in the psalm at 2.5 (ET 2.6) and in the prose at 1.3, 5. While he admits that the psalm is very similar to other psalms, he tries to show that this merely represents traditional psalm language which is used by the author in the first part of the psalm to obtain a familiar framework against which to contrast his own original material. He points out that towards the end of the psalm the familiar language falls away and the author creates his own description. Magonet believes that this movement from the familiar to the unfamiliar is deliberate and is reflected in the book as a whole where familiar views of God and pagans are given a twist.

Magonet argues that the 'inappropriateness' of the psalm disappears if the ironic nature of the book is properly understood. Jonah may be inconsistent, but that is the kind of picture given of him elsewhere in the book. Again, thanksgiving is not out of place at this point because the author depicts Jonah as anticipating being restored to dry land. Magonet describes the author as 'an excellent midrashist'; and one wonders if there is a touch of admiration in this observation!

Landes' views, on the other hand, are not so difficult to accept as those of Magonet. He takes the view that the psalm originally had a separate existence but was chosen and placed here by the author of the book. He believes that the words 'and he prayed...fish' (2.2; ET 2.1) refer not to the psalm but to a prayer of confession and supplication, a prayer which is not supplied by the author, and that this prayer is alluded to in the psalm at 2.8 (ET 2.7).

Jonah 4.5

Second only to the appropriateness of the psalm of ch. 2 is the question of the position of 4.5. The book of Jonah is, on the whole, a well-written story; but even a casual reader is bound to be curious about the statement at 4.5 that 'Jonah went out of the city and sat down to the east of the city, and made a booth for himself there. He sat under it in the shade, till he should see what would become of the city'. The question immediately arises: did not Jonah already know that Nineveh had repented and that God was not going to carry out his threat (3.10)? Indeed, was not that the reason for Jonah's anger (3.10–4.3)? Why should he now go out to see? The passage is also problematic because of the verses which follow. From v. 6 to the end of the book nothing more is said as to what happens in the city or to the city. In fact, as Trible points out, Nineveh is referred to in v. 11 because of what *had* happened there (3.10–4.3), not as the locus of any subsequent activity.

Another question arises over 4.5 even for the casual reader, and that is the question of the booth which Jonah erects for shade. In the very next verse God causes a plant to grow for the same purpose, and at v. 8 Jonah has *only* the plant; no further mention is made of the booth! It would seem, then, that 4.5 is doubly difficult. The problem has long been noticed, and in mediaeval times (for instance in the commentaries by Kimchi and Ibn Ezra) the suggestion was made that we should understand the verbs of the verse as having a

5. The Integrity of the Book 35

pluperfect sense: 'Jonah *had* gone out of the city and *had*...'; and this is a view which has some support today (van der Woude, Lohfink). The implication of this interpretation would be that 4.5 refers back to the time before Nineveh repents, that is, the period between the events of 3.4, where Jonah preaches, and 3.5, when Nineveh repents. It has been argued in this connection that the author did not place it in the latter position because that would have broken the flow of the narrative. Those who are unconvinced by the 'pluperfect' solution—and it is debatable whether one may translate the verbs in this sense (the RSV, REB, JB and NIV translators do not appear to accept it)—may be divided into two groups: those who retain 4.5 in its present position, and those who suggest that it originally belonged after 3.4.

Those who feel that the verse is in its correct position but who do not believe that it refers back to the period between 3.4 and 3.5 have the difficulty of explaining (1) why Jonah is still waiting for something to happen, and (2) the juxtaposition of booth and plant; Jonah still hopes that the destruction of the city will take place, either because the Ninevites had not truly repented and would return to their evil ways, or because God, who has angered Jonah, will change tack again and carry out the threat. The booth withered after a time or was blown away by the wind, but in any case it provided inadequate shade for Jonah.

Magonet is convinced that there is no real problem here. He argues that, in the light of the structure of ch. 4, Jonah's leaving the city is a direct answer to God's question in v. 4; it is a reply in action. One element in this 'answer' is Jonah's erecting a booth and his concern for his own comfort. God replies with action. He picks up the theme of comfort and increases Jonah's comfort by creating a shady plant. What God is saying in this action-reply is: 'You are more concerned with your comfort than with a city full of people—very well, let us see what the implications of your concern are'. Jonah goes on then to experience first the comfort of the shade and then the pain when the plant withers. Thus, just as Jonah's flight to sea was 'answered' by God by means of a storm at sea, so here too God allows Jonah's choice of action to dictate his method of reply. When we recognize this, the full significance of God's choice of the plant as a means of teaching Jonah a lesson becomes apparent.

Many scholars during the last hundred years have adopted the suggestion that 4.5 has been misplaced and that it originally stood after 3.4. It is claimed that transposing 4.5 to this position solves the problem. Jonah then naturally sits down to wait after delivering his message, and the result is given in the verses which follow. The problem of the booth still remains, however, although less acutely. Now the booth and the plant are separated in time, and one may perhaps imagine that the booth was a very temporary structure which was replaced by the plant. But this is not really a satisfactory answer to the problem of 4.5. Apart from the fact that there is neither manuscript nor versional support for the transposition, the problem of there being first a booth and then a plant does not really go away.

It may be that we are dealing with a story which has had a long history and that an earlier form of it contained a reference to a booth but not a plant, a reference which was not deleted when the plant episode became attached. Again, if the transposition is a correct suggestion how did the corruption occur? Was it a scribal error? If so, it had already occurred before any translation was made. If the verse was deliberately placed after 4.4 could it be that it was felt that some response to God's question of 4.4 was needed, much as a psalm was thought to be appropriate at 2.2 (or 2.10)?

Van der Woude has an interesting explanation of the two problems. Picking up the 'pluperfect' suggestion, he argues that we ought to translate 4.5a 'Jonah had gone out of the city and had sat to the east of the city' (cf. MLB and NJV). Further 'pluperfect' examples are to be found in Jonah at 2.1 (ET 1.17), 'The LORD had appointed a great fish...', and at 3.6, 'The news had reached the king of Nineveh...'. In the former passage it makes good sense to translate in this way, although very few modern translations agree (exceptions being JB and MLB). In the latter passage the pluperfect interpretation, indicating a flashback (cf. 1.5b, 10b), removes the difficulty that the people repent and don sackcloth before the

5. *The Integrity of the Book* 37

king of Nineveh issues a decree encouraging them to do so. Van der Woude then translates 5b, 'There he had *wanted* to build a booth for himself and had *wanted* to sit under it till...city'. The main parallel to 5b in the Old Testament would be Gen. 37.21, 'But when Reuben heard it he delivered him out of their hands...', which ought (according to van der Woude) to be translated, 'But when Reuben heard it he *wanted* to deliver him out of their hands' (because the deliverance was still to come). Van der Woude, following Saydon, argues that this sense is also to be found in 1 Kgs 9.23; 20.1; Jer. 37.12; 2 Chron. 14.5. If his interpretation is correct, the problem of the juxtaposition of booth and plant melts away, for Jonah only *intends* to build a booth; it is still on the drawing-board when God produces the plant! Perhaps this is why the author places the statement at this point—when the plant is about to be provided.

Divine Names

It was inevitable that the criteria which served Pentateuchal criticism should be employed in other parts of the Old Testament and in particular that the findings in Pentateuchal study should influence the critical study of the prophets. Commentaries on the prophetic literature are strewn with observations which raise questions of plurality of authorship, editorial activity and so on.

One of the phenomena lying behind the earliest Pentateuchal criticism is the use of different names for God. But although in the case of the Pentateuch this observation was useful and helpful it has not been a prominent tool in the study of other parts of the Old Testament. It is interesting, however, to note that there is a variation in the names of God used by the author of Jonah. This is not clear to the reader of most English translations where the variation is camouflaged. The word 'Lord' has been substituted, out of reverence for the holy name; hence in English translations, apart from the Jerusalem Bible where *Yahweh* is actually used, the rendering LORD is to be found.

In the Hebrew text of Jonah the variation in the appellations of God is clearly observable. In 1.1–2.3 the name *yhwh* ('LORD' in English Bibles) is used; in 3.5-10 the word *ᵉlōhim* ('God') is used; in 4.1-4 it is *yhwh* again; in 4.6 it is a combination, *yhwh ᵉlōhim* ('LORD God' in English; cf. Gen. 2.4); in 4.7-9 it is *ᵉlōhim* again; and in 4.10 it is *yhwh*. While in English one may use the terms 'Lord' and 'God' interchangeably, this is not quite the case in Hebrew; and a careful reading of the relevant passages in Jonah reveals that, for the most part, these variations can be accounted for. Thus in 1.1–2.3 it is perhaps natural that the author should use the divine name *yhwh*, referring to Israel's and Jonah's God. In 3.5-10 the scene is of the Ninevites repenting and, although for the author *yhwh* equals 'God', he is not here describing a conversion to a cult of Yahweh. The reversion to *yhwh* in 4.1-4 will have seemed natural to our author since here the narrative has to do with Jonah again.

But in 4.6-10 the variations are not so easy to explain. For example, 'LORD God' in 4.6, 'God' in 4.7-9 and 'LORD' in 4.10 appear to be variations within a section where the focus is on Yahweh and Jonah. Attempts at explaining this have not been successful, and it may well be that the concerns mentioned above have been only at the back of the author's mind, and that he became inconsistent towards the end of the story. It is possible that the variations at this point are the result of editorial activity, but the motivation for alteration such as from 'God' to 'LORD God' is not easy to discern. In any event there does not seem to be any reason to suppose that the variations in the divine name suggest that different sources are involved, although there has been argument for this view, beginning in 1887 with Böhme.

Conclusion

The question of the integrity of the book is, therefore, not an easy one. Students should consult the Further Reading lists, and it might be best to begin with Kraeling's article. My own view is that the original story did not contain the psalm; and that the original text read, 'Then Jonah prayed to the Lord from the belly of the fish. And the Lord spoke to the fish, and

5. The Integrity of the Book

it vomited out Jonah upon the dry land'. In the course of transmission the psalm was written in the margin of a manuscript by a scribe who intended it to refer to the deliverance of Jonah on his return to dry land, that is, as a song of thanksgiving. A later copyist incorporated the psalm into the text but not at the point for which it was intended. When I began to examine 4.5 my initial conviction was that it had been misplaced and belongs after 3.4; but I am now inclined to the view that 4.5 is a flashback to the period after Jonah's announcement of doom. Van der Woude's suggestion that we ought to translate 'He wanted to make a booth for himself there' is attractive (and it would solve a lot of problems at a stroke); but I feel that he is asking too much of the Hebrew text here. The issue of divine names still remains a problem. Although it is surely the case that the author was consciously and carefully using each name, the anomalies in 4.6-10 are puzzling. It would, however, be going too far to conclude that a plurality of sources underlies the passage.

Further Reading

Allen, *The Books of Joel, Obadiah, Jonah and Micah*.
Bewer, *A Critical and Exegetical Commentary on Haggai, Zechariah, Malachi and Jonah*, pp. 21-24.
W. Böhme, 'Die Composition des Buches Jona', *ZAW* 7 (1887), pp. 224-84.
J. Day, 'Problems in the Interpretation of the Book of Jonah', *OS* 26 (1990), pp. 32-47, 40-42.
W.M.L. De Wette, *A Critical and Historical Introduction to the Canonical Scriptures of the Old Testament*, II (Boston: Little, Brown, 2nd edn, 1850), pp. 451-56.
S.D. Goitein, 'Some Observations on Jonah', *JPOS* 17 (1937), pp. 33-77.
F.W. Kidner, 'The Distribution of the Divine Names in Jonah', *TynBul* 21 (1970), pp. 126-28.
E.G. Kraeling, 'The Evolution of the Story of Jonah', in *Hommages à A. Dupont-Sommer* (Paris: Andrien–Maisonneuve, 1971), pp. 305-18.
G.M. Landes, 'The Kerygma of the Book of Jonah', *Int* 21 (1967), pp. 3-31.
N. Lohfink, 'Jona ging zur Stadt hinaus (Jon. 4, 5)', *BZ* 5 (1961), pp. 185-203.
Magonet, *Form and Meaning*.
P.P. Saydon, 'The Conative Imperfect in Hebrew', *VT* 12 (1962), pp. 124-26.
Smart, 'Jonah', pp. 873-74.

Sasson, *Jonah*, pp. 287-90.
Trible, 'Studies in the Book of Jonah', pp. 75-82.
W. Tyndale, 'The Prologue to the Prophet Jonas', in D. Daniell (ed.), *Tyndale's Old Testament, Being the Pentateuch of 1530, Joshua to 2 Chronicles of 1537, and Jonah* (New Haven and London: Yale University Press, 1992).
Wade, *Micah, Obadiah, Joel and Jonah*, pp. lxxxv-vi.
Wolff, *Obadiah and Jonah*, pp. 128-31, 169.
A.S. van der Woude, 'Nachholende Erzählung im Buche Jona', in A. Rofé and Y. Zakowitch (eds.), *Essays on the Bible and the Ancient World (I.L. Seeligmann Volume)*, III (Jerusalem: E. Rubenstein, 1983), pp. 267-72.

6
GENRE

WHILE IT IS CLEAR THAT the book differs from other prophetic books in the Old Testament it is not clear how it should be classified. In the Old Testament there is history writing, legend, parable, lament, song and more, and attempts have been made to place Jonah in one or other of these categories. This is an important question, more important than it might seem at first, for the interpretation of the book depends on the intention of the author in this regard.

History

It is perhaps surprising that Jonah is still classified as history by some Old Testament scholars, but this has been argued as late as 1985 (Alexander). This stance is, however, due in general not to a scientific study of the material as such but to a doctrinal position which controls a particular view of Scripture; so that anything found in the Bible, it is believed, is almost bound to be factual. Luther's remark on Jonah and the fish, 'Who would believe it...if it were not in the Bible?', demonstrates this. Indeed, the history of the interpretation of Jonah is littered with painful efforts to stand by this position. The credibility of events in the book, particularly that of the fish swallowing Jonah, became the touchstone of faith, and von Rad relates that in the eighteenth century a professor of theology in Germany was fined 100 florins and forbidden to teach because he dared to question the historical nature of the book. In the middle of the last century E.B. Pusey devoted several paragraphs of his commentary on the book to an investigation of the kind of fish which could swallow an adult human being. This doctrinal position is also firmly supported, if not initiated, by the references in the New Testament to Jonah; since Jesus spoke of Jonah in the belly of the fish it follows that he believed the book to be a historical work. It is an interesting and surprising fact that the fish incident which has so exercised and dominated interpreters' minds for centuries is mentioned in only three verses out of the 48 of the book!

At first sight it seems easy to dismiss these arguments. While it appears to be the case that a prophet Jonah ben Amittai was active in Israel in the eighth century BCE, while Joppa, Nineveh and Tarshish were real places in Old Testament times, other features of the book do not seem credible. It is not just the matter of a fish swallowing a man and regurgitating him unharmed after three days, after he had composed a psalm to boot. There are other problems. How could the sailors speak Hebrew and pray in Old Testament terms? How could the casting of lots sort matters out? How could it be known that the storm ceased and that the sailors then were afraid and sacrificed? Jonah might have been able to relate most of what appears in the book, but while he was asleep and after his departure from the boat he was not a witness. How could the Ninevites understand Jonah? How could Nineveh be so large as to require three days to cross? Is it credible that a whole city—every single person—could repent? Not even an American TV evangelist could command such success! Furthermore, no mention is made of the Assyrians as such; nor does the name 'Israel' occur in the book. Surely this is not history! As Bewer says, 'We are in wonderland'.

It might, however, be countered that there are parts of the Deuteronomistic history which do not bear rigorous historical investigation, and which can be shown to lack historicity. Joshua 1–11, for example, gives the impression that Joshua arranged for the death of everything that breathed in Canaan; this was clearly not the case, yet it seems to be presented as history. It seems to have been the writer's intention to describe the past. Could this be said of the author of Jonah? If it could, can the book be classified as anything other than history? As Alexander argues,

6. Genre

even if we could demonstrate beyond all doubt that an event recorded in Jonah never took place, this of itself, would not prove that the author himself did not view the event as historical. It is the author's intention, not historical probability or accuracy which is decisive for determining the nature of the work.

The implication here is that all the attacks on the book which scoff at its historical credibility are irrelevant to the argument. If the author thought he was describing the past, the nature of his work is on a par with that of the Deuteronomist.

Hence the question is: did the author *think* he was recording events in the past? It is impossible to know, but there are indications that he did *not* intend to record the past. To begin with, he does not give the book a particular historical setting. While it might be argued that the reader would have knowledge of the information given in 2 Kings, where Jonah the prophet is mentioned, the fact that the author gets the area of Nineveh wrong, that he uses the term 'king of Nineveh' when there could not have been such an office in Jeroboam's time, and that he does not name the king, points very firmly to the conclusion that he was simply not interested in a particular period of history; and there are no other points of historical contact in the book. Furthermore, a genuine historian would surely state the bald facts in sequence, stating at the outset why Jonah did not want to preach to Nineveh, indicating Jonah's whereabouts when he found himself back on dry land and perhaps giving some indication of the route he took to Nineveh.

One cannot be dogmatic about these matters, and the debate will continue, though I fear the sides will draw farther apart as respect for one another's position diminishes. But, as Fretheim points out, even if we solved the underlying problems, 'the question of the message of the book has at that point hardly begun to be discerned'.

Fable

One definition of 'fable' is 'a narration not founded on fact, a fabrication'. The term is used in scholarly circles for stories such as Elijah's meal jar and cruse of oil, and the story of the ravens; or the story of Balaam's talking ass (Num. 22.22-35). One can imagine Philo's opponents in Alexandria scoffing at the book of Jonah and dismissing it as a fable of this type. Indeed, Eissfeldt classifies the first part of the book in this way. There are some features of the book which invite this classification, such as God's speaking to the fish which swallows Jonah, and the involvement of animals in the acts of repentance; but it is now generally felt that while the author made use of folklore motifs in the construction of his work, he has arranged the whole in such a way that it goes beyond the folklore genre.

It should, however, be noted that the term 'fable' is given another definition in the *OED*, that is, 'a short story devised to convey some useful lesson'. Perhaps on this definition Jonah has a stronger claim to this classification, although because of the dominance of the first definition of 'fable' it is perhaps best avoided.

Allegory

The view that the book of Jonah is an allegory is not much in vogue, although it does occasionally raise its head, Rowley and Ackroyd being its latest exponents. Philo of Alexandria indulged in this method of exegesis in the face of Hellenistic philosophers who ridiculed the Hebrew Scriptures because, *inter alia*, of fantastic stories, such as Jonah's being swallowed by the fish. According to this view Jonah represents Israel, the three days and nights in the fish symbolize the exile in Babylon, his disobedience the sin of Israel; his return to dry land suggests return from exile, with the task of leading the heathen to God. As Miller Burrows says, 'The history of exegesis affords abundant proof that an ingenious interpreter can treat any narrative as an allegory and make it mean almost anything he wishes'.

But there are obstacles to this classification of Jonah. Feuillet notes that the fish is a vehicle of deliverance, not of punishment; and Jonah's asking the sailors to throw him

6. *Genre* 45

overboard does not quite lend itself to this method of interpretation.

Legend

It has been pointed out that the formula with which the book begins, 'The word of the LORD came to...saying...', although similar to those at the beginning of the books of Joel and Micah, is *exactly* the same as in the legendary stories about Elijah, Elishah and other prophetic figures. The question is, therefore: could the story of Jonah be of similar genre? Could it be a legend about the prophet? It is certainly tempting, for these reasons, to classify it in this way, and literary qualities claimed for the work need not militate against this view; a legend can be entertaining and gripping.

The student should, perhaps, consult Gunkel's work on legend at this juncture. Although legend is not history, it is not unrelated to history; indeed, its roots lie in history despite the fact that the point of departure may have been embellished and overlaid with miracle and myth. There is not much which might be considered historical fact in Jonah, although the names Tarshish, Joppa and Nineveh are real enough, and Nineveh had the reputation of being evil (cf. the book of Nahum). The only other link to history is the name Jonah ben Amittai (1.1). It is possible that the prophet who is mentioned in 2 Kgs 14.27 had uttered an oracle against Nineveh at some point in his career and that a story grew up around it. Some scholars argue that Jonah is depicted in 2 Kgs 14.27 as a nationalistic prophet, supporting Jeroboam's expansionist policy, and that a legend grew up around this issue: Jonah represents nationalism, unwilling to preach to non-Israelite Nineveh. This may be going beyond the evidence, however, for it is not at all clear that Jonah is given such an image in Kings.

Certain other features of the book would satisfy the characteristics of legend. Thus what Gunkel sees as a necessary ingredient, sustained interest throughout, is true of Jonah. In legend we find a simple portrayal of characters. Few people are involved and often they depict types rather than individuals: Jonah is a type of disobedient servant, the sailor is a type of pagan, Nineveh is a type of evil city, the king a type of great ruler. Although an original historical fact may lie behind the story, the embellishments are economic. We are not given a date, we are not told what wickedness existed in Nineveh; we do not know whether Jonah prayed when asked to do so by the captain of the ship; the vows of the sailors are not specified; the location of the dry land where Jonah was deposited is not given, nor is his subsequent route to Nineveh. We are not told the king's name or what befell Jonah afterwards.

The problem, however, with applying the term 'legend' to Jonah is that in legendary material there is generally a historical figure whose exploits, possibly exaggerated, as here perhaps, are lauded, and the figure becomes a kind of hero or model whom the reader is encouraged to emulate. With Jonah this is not the case. Jonah is presented as a rather negative character, and although he features all the way through the story it is God who speaks at the beginning and the end, and his final words are a question which Jonah is not permitted, by the author, to answer. Indeed, it might be said that the book is about God's dealings with Jonah (as suggested by Wolff). Eissfeldt's suggestion that there may have existed a story about a protest of Jonah's against a commission by God, which has been developed in a way similar to the development of a story about Elijah (1 Kgs 19.4-8), is possible; but while the story may have originated in this way, the book as we have it has a different ring to it.

Parable

Bewer, Allen and others classify the book as a parable. Although the *OED* gives 'an allegory' as one meaning of this term, it is more generally understood in the light of the parables of Jesus, that is, as 'a fictitious narrative (usually of something which might naturally occur) by which moral or spiritual relations are typically set forth'. Since the story of Jonah is not something which would naturally occur it may be that this definition does not fit here either. Furthermore, quite apart from the difference in length between the New Testament parables and the book of Jonah, the fact that the latter begins with an actual person who converses with God would seem to put it on a different plane, since none of the parables of Jesus identifies a figure in the story.

Midrash

This is a Hebrew word meaning 'explanation'. In 2 Chron. 24.27 there is a reference to a work to which the Chronicler had access but which is no longer extant, the midrash or commentary on the book of Kings. It may be that in this document the reference to Jonah ben Amittai in 2 Kgs 14.25 occasioned some comments; we cannot say. However, some scholars argue that the book of Jonah is, in fact, a commentary on that verse in Kings and that it originally stood in the commentary referred to in 2 Chron. 24.27.

A variation of this view is that the book may be a midrash on Jer. 18.8: 'If that nation, concerning which I have spoken, turns from its evil, I will repent of the evil that I intended to do to it', while another variation takes as the point of departure Exod. 34.6: 'the Lord, a God merciful and gracious, slow to anger and abounding in steadfast love and faithfulness', seeing the book of Jonah as a midrash on that verse.

There is no doubt that the book of Jonah has connections with these passages; but, as we have seen, it also has links with other parts of the Old Testament, for instance with Joel 2.13. Furthermore, the term 'midrash' is a complex one. It may be that the term was applied at different times to a number of different styles of 'comment'; but if the student were to open the Midrash Rabbah on, say, Genesis, the impression obtained would hardly correspond to that taken from a reading of the book of Jonah. In the Midrash Rabbah the text or passage which is being discussed (often homiletically) is specifically alluded to again and again. If one were to extract a full narrative from such literature it would, even in isolation, be quite obvious which passage it was intended to illustrate or explain. In the case of the book of Jonah this is not at all obvious.

Didactic Story

Stories about prophets—that is, stories about well-known events in the lives of the prophets—were fairly common in Israel. While they varied in length (those about Amos, Isaiah and Hosea are quite short, while those about Samuel and Elijah are slightly longer) von Rad argues that we can speak about a fixed literary genre as a traditional narrative form. If we compare the beginning of the book of Jonah with the way other prophetic stories begin (for instance 1 Sam. 15.10; 1 Kgs 17.2) we can see a similarity. So perhaps this is how the book of Jonah began. But it is not simply a story about a prophet, for the author is not, as in other cases, concerned with God's word being fulfilled by means of a prophet, but with a rebellious prophet, and with one oracle which is *not* fulfilled. Furthermore, whereas the stories about other prophets have clear endings this is not the case with Jonah. The reader is left wondering what the outcome was in the dialogue between Jonah and God.

We are, therefore, dealing with a development of the prophetic narrative; a development which aims, in various ways, to teach. The unanswered question at 4.11 underlines this. The readers are invited to question their own theology in the light of the foregoing. Hence 'didactic story' seems to be the most appropriate classification. No one doubts that it is a story (true or false); furthermore, even those who argue for the historicity of the story will allow that the author's intention is to teach his readers.

Further Reading

General

Allen, *The Books of Joel, Obadiah, Jonah and Micah*, pp. 175-81.

T.D. Alexander, 'Jonah and Genre', *TynBul* 36 (1985), pp. 35-59.

M.E. Andrew, 'Gattung and Intention of the Book of Jonah', *Orita* 1 (1967), pp. 13-18, 78-85.

Day, 'Problems in the Interpretation of the Book of Jonah', pp. 32-39.

E.B. Pusey, *The Minor Prophets* (Oxford: J.H. and J. Parker, 1869), pp. 247-87.

Sasson, *Jonah*, pp. 321-52.

Wolff, *Obadiah and Jonah*, pp. 80-85.

6. Genre

History

G.C. Aalders, *The Problem of the Book of Jonah* (London: Tyndale Press, 1948).

Alexander, 'Jonah and Genre', pp. 35-59.

D.W.B. Robinson, 'Jonah', in D. Guthrie and J.A. Motyer (eds.), *New Bible Commentary Revised* (London: Inter-Varsity Press, 1970), pp. 746-51.

B. Trépanier, 'The Story of Jonas', *CBQ* 13 (1951), pp. 8-16.

J. Walton, *Jonah* (Grand Rapids: Zondervan, 1982).

Allegory

P.R. Ackroyd, *Exile and Restoration* (London: SCM Press, 1968), pp. 244-45.

A.R. Johnson, 'Jonah 2.3-10: A Study in Cultic Phantasy', in H.H. Rowley (ed.), *Studies in Old Testament Prophecy* (Edinburgh: T. & T. Clark, 1950), pp. 82-102.

G.A.F. Knight, *Ruth and Jonah* (London: SCM Press, 1950).

A.D. Martin, *The Prophet Jonah: The Book and the Sign* (London: Longmans, Green & Co., 1926).

G.A. Smith, *The Book of the Twelve Prophets*, II (London: Hodder & Stoughton, 1895).

C.H.H. Wright, *Biblical Essays* (Edinburgh: T. & T. Clark, 1886), pp. 34-98.

Midrash

Brockington, 'Jonah', pp. 627-29.

K. Budde, 'Vermutungen zum "Midrash des Buches der Könige"', *ZAW* 11 (1892), pp. 37-51.

E. Nielsen, 'Le message primitif du livre de Jonas', *RHPR* 59 (1979), p. 502.

Trible, 'Studies in the Book of Jonah'.

The student should, perhaps, also consult A.G. Wright, 'The Literary Genre Midrash', *CBQ* 28 (1966), pp. 105-38, 417-57.

Parable

Allen, *The Books of Joel, Obadiah, Jonah and Micah*.

Bewer, *A Critical and Exegetical Commentary on Haggai, Zechariah, Malachi and Jonah*.

Smart, *Jonah*, p. 872.

Watts, *The Books of Joel, Obadiah, Jonah, Nahum, Habakkuk and Zephaniah*.

Legend

O. Eissfeldt, *The Old Testament: An Introduction* (Oxford: Basil Blackwell, 1974), pp. 403-406.

C.-A. Keller, 'Jonas', in E. Jacob, C.-A. Keller and S. Amsler, *Osée, Joel, Abdias, Jonas, Amos* (Neuchâtel: Delachaux & Niestlé, 1965).
The student should also consult H. Gunkel, *The Legends of Genesis* (New York: Schocken Books, 1964).

Novella
Andrew, 'Gattung and Intention of the Book of Jonah', pp. 13-18, 78-85.
O. Kaiser, *Introduction to the Old Testament* (Oxford: Basil Blackwell, 1975), pp. 194-98.
G.M. Landes, 'Jonah', *IDBSup*, pp. 488-91.
Wolff, *Obadiah and Jonah*, pp. 82-85.

Satire
J.S. Ackerman, 'Jonah', in R. Alter and F. Kermode (eds.), *The Literary Guide to the Old Testament* (London: Collins, 1987), pp. 234-43.
Andrew, 'Gattung and Intention of the Book of Jonah', pp. 13-18, 78-85.
M. Burrows, 'The Literary Category of the Book of Jonah', in H.T. Frank and W.L. Reed (eds.), *Translating and Understanding the Old Testament: Essays in Honor of Herbert Gordon May* (Nashville: Abingdon Press, 1970), pp. 80-107.

Didactic Short Story
T.E. Fretheim, *The Message of Jonah* (Minneapolis: Augsburg, 1977).
A. Feuillet, 'Le sens du livre de Jonas', *RB* 54 (1947), pp. 340-61.
G. von Rad, *Old Testament Theology*, II (Edinburgh and London: Oliver & Boyd, 1965), p. 291.
—'The Prophet Jonah', in *God at Work in Israel* (Nashville: Abingdon Press, 1974), pp. 58-70.

7
THE PURPOSE OF THE BOOK

I HAVE ALREADY ALLUDED to the links which Jonah has with the rest of the Old Testament while, at the same time, underlining the differences. We can deduce, from what has been said, something of how the narrator thinks, his theology, his background, his beliefs and his presuppositions; and *most* of these have parallels in other parts of the Hebrew Bible. In trying to ascertain the author's purpose, therefore, we should scrutinize the areas in which he differs from other parts of Scripture. The author of Jonah is not responsible for the book's position among the Minor Prophets nor, indeed, for its inclusion in the Hebrew canon, but it is generally agreed, even by those who are in considerable disagreement about the book's date and provenance, that the author, while a skilful storyteller, is not simply telling a story but is, by means of a story, trying to convey a message (perhaps more than one message) to his audience or readers. Discussion and disagreement over the integrity and provenance of the book does not preclude our investigating what this message might be.

The separation of purpose from themes that occur in the book is not simple. Several themes raise their heads from time to time. There is the theme of the rebellious prophet who tries to avoid Yahweh's commission but who is forced to conform and to complete the task. The call of Yahweh is irresistible. Then there is the theme of Yahweh as creator. He sends the storm, commands the fish to swallow and deposit Jonah, causes the plant to grow, arranges for the worm to attack the plant and calls up the east wind. Yahweh is in control of nature. Again, the theme of repentance is important, although not in the first part of the book. The Ninevites fully repent, and Yahweh repents of the threatened disaster. Finally there is the theme of the mercy and compassion of Yahweh. Yahweh is very patient and long-suffering with Jonah, and has mercy on the sailors and the Ninevites; indeed, it might be argued that Yahweh's absolute sovereign freedom is the author's ultimate concern. Even the sailors are made to utter 'thou, O Lord, hast done as it pleased thee' (1.14).

Early Interpretations

One of the earliest interpretations of the book was that Jonah, knowing with prophetic insight that Nineveh would repent and be delivered, was reluctant to carry out his mission since the end result would be to bring great shame upon his own people, Israel. (This interpretation was picked up by the Christian church and used to denigrate the Jews.) His refusal and flight having been thwarted and the mission accomplished, Israel was being shown what the hated Ninevites could do. The view was, then, that the book was written to show an example to Israel. The mediaeval Jewish commentator Kimchi wrote: 'This prophecy was written for instruction to Israel' (1.1). It was also stressed that Jonah's reluctance was not due to lack of faith, but to his faith in his own people, and that this is the reason that God was not angry with Jonah in the story.

Some Christian commentators tended to interpret the book so as to support anti-Jewish feelings. They could point to the passage in Matthew's gospel (12.41): 'the men of Nineveh will arise at the judgment with this generation and condemn it; for they repented at the preaching of Jonah'; and this was, to some extent, a control on their thinking. Some Gentile Christian churches saw themselves represented by Nineveh in the story—accepted by God. They pointed out that Jonah was not angry for the sake of Israel but because the Ninevites, that is, Gentiles, were to be the object of God's love and forgiveness. It was argued that Jonah represented the narrow-

7. The Purpose of the Book

minded Israelites who disagreed with the salvation of the Gentiles.

Not all Christians were of this opinion; Jerome, for example, opposed it. He believed that the purpose of the book was to encourage the Jews to repent. The fact that Jonah's three days and three nights in the fish had been thought to prefigure the period between the crucifixion and resurrection of Jesus (Mt. 12.40) suggested to some that Jonah was a type of Christ, and so the association with narrow-mindedness was played down. Indeed, in the mediaeval period, the tendency was to support the view that Jonah had been zealous for his own people, Israel, and was not opposed to the Ninevites per se.

But Luther revived the old view that Jonah was actively opposed to the Ninevites, that is, Gentiles, and to their salvation; for him, Jonah represents narrow-minded Israel, the Jews who were to reject Jesus Christ; and this view was widely shared by later thinkers. Calvin, however, insisted that Jonah's reluctance to travel to Nineveh was because he did not want to be known as a false prophet. He anticipated proclaiming a message of doom which would not be realized.

Present-Day Interpretations

Universalism
There are some commentators today who have tended towards the view that the purpose of the book and the message of its author is that of universalism. It is argued that God's mercy and forgiveness, having been extended towards Israel, are here seen as also extended towards the Gentiles, represented by the Ninevites. This change derives from creation theology: if God is the creator of all things he is the creator of all peoples and nations, and his concern must be for them as well as for Israel. The *reaction* to this view is represented in the story by Jonah himself—a member of the establishment. It is that God ought only to be interested in Israel. These two concerns are clearly drawn in the book. A narrow view which believes that God is only interested in Israel is treated negatively in that Jonah is disobedient, is a reluctant prophet, is unhappy and angry even after a completely successful mission to Nineveh,

and, in the final scene, argues sulkily with God. By contrast, the pagans are treated positively. The sailors, a varied group with different religious and national backgrounds, are depicted as sincere and positive people. They pray as they know how, they try their best to save the ship even when they suspect that Jonah has brought trouble on them and are advised by him to cast him overboard, they are very reluctant to sacrifice his life and will only do so as a last resort, and when they have prayed to God. Later they sacrifice to God and make vows. The Ninevites are also given a positive treatment, apart from the early allusion to their great evil. Immediately on hearing Jonah's preaching they believe God, they repent *en masse* and everyone puts on sackcloth and fasts, trusting in God's mercy. In the final speech God cites their helplessness and ignorance as further reasons for his concern for them. The contrast between Jonah's attitude and that of the pagans is very clear in the book and must be taken into account on any interpretation of Jonah.

The universalistic interpretation is itself not without variations. Some scholars, endeavouring to discover the historical locus of the book, understand the message to be directed at the situation in the days of Ezra and Nehemiah when intermarriage with pagans was frowned upon and forbidden. The author of Jonah is seen therefore as opposed to such measures, and his book is meant to provide, in narrative form, a theology which undermines them. Another variation on the universalistic theme, represented by Rowley, is that the book was written to encourage missionary zeal. The author, he argues, is describing his own experiences. He himself was reluctant to believe that God's love embraced alien peoples, even oppressors like Assyria, and he had resisted this idea. But he came to believe that God was the God of all and that the faith of Israel was to be shared by all. He went beyond those who dreamed of the day when all would worship God. He realized that messengers of grace were needed. This missionary voice is not acted upon in the Old Testament but the message is clear enough. Rowley's observations have had very little following, and the majority of 'universalists' take a much broader view of the book.

7. The Purpose of the Book 55

One of the problems in interpreting the book is the author's choice of the eighth-century BCE prophet Jonah ben Amittai as the subject of the story. Although nothing is known about Jonah except for the passage in 2 Kgs 14.23-25, it is thought, by some universalists, that this is enough to brand Jonah as a nationalistic prophet, and that this is the reason why his name was used by the author. Jonah was, therefore, opposed to foreign nations. It is further argued (as I have noted above) that the author cited the prophet Joel, and that what we have here represents a response by the author to Joel. Because Joel (with other passages of the Old Testament which are reflected in Jon. 4.2) praises the mercy of Yahweh towards Israel while the book of Jonah extends this mercy to include Ninevites, it is argued that Jonah is a response to Joel. Since Joel uttered oracles of judgment against foreign nations (Joel 4.1-21; ET 3.1-21) Jonah could be a reaction to the fierceness of the thinking represented by Joel. This latter view was espoused by Hitzig, Feuillet and more recently by Day.

Non-Universalism

Those scholars who are opposed to deriving a universalistic message from Jonah argue that this is to read into the text the experiences of a later age. On the question of the missionary interpretation it is pointed out that the sailors, although they sacrifice and vow to God, are not depicted as abandoning their own gods, nor as becoming devotees of the cult of Yahweh; nor do the Ninevites abandon idolatry when they repent of their evil deeds. While the name of Yahweh is used by the sailors (though not by the Ninevites), there is no specific mention of Israelites nor of the fact that Yahweh is the God of Israel. (Indeed the fact that the words 'Israel' and 'Gentiles' are not to be found anywhere in the book may be a weakness in the universalist argument.) The linking of the message with the era of Ezra and Nehemiah has also come in for criticism. Jonah sounds very different in tone from Ezra or Nehemiah, and there is no evidence in the book of a particular group or party being criticized, no mention of mixed marriages, no explicit contrast between Jews and pagans.

As mentioned above, Calvin understood the story to be

about Jonah not wanting to appear as a false prophet. There is little evidence that other scholars followed this line of thinking but, more recently, the view has been expressed again. Emmerson and others argue that there is nothing in the book which is anti-pagan, that Jonah never expresses opposition to paganism or even to the evil of the Ninevites. It is wrong to take Jonah as representing Israel and Nineveh as representing the Gentiles. The story is meant to express the absolute freedom of Yahweh and the dilemma of a prophet who has been given a categorical message from Yahweh, and who first of all fears that it will not be fulfilled and then discovers that his fears were well founded. Jonah is angry not at the Ninevites but at Yahweh. The clue is found at 3.10: 'When God saw what they did, how they turned from their evil way, God repented of the evil which he had said he would do to them; and he did not do it'. The final chapter then deals with Jonah's emotions. Jonah is capable of emotion about the plant; how much more is Yahweh concerned about the helpless!

Emmerson is almost persuasive. But while Nineveh may not mean much to the present-day reader, it surely meant something to the author of the book and to the ancient reader. It is not enough to treat Nineveh as though it were Megiddo, and any interpretation which fails to see significance in Nineveh is, perhaps, suspect.

Another interpretation worthy of consideration is that of Kaufmann. He holds that the book was written in the eighth century and has nothing to do with Israel's quarrel with the Gentiles. He points out that the kind of 'universalism' present in Jonah is not unlike that found in early Old Testament narratives: God is concerned with the nations in the flood story and in the Sodom story and punishes them for their misdeeds; there is the fear of God in Abimelech, King of Gerar, in Genesis 20 (compare also the Egyptian midwives in Exod. 1.15-21 who are described as God-fearing). So it is not unique in the Old Testament to find in Jonah that the pagans are depicted as fearing God. Kaufmann argues that the significance of the book comes out clearly in ch. 4, where Jonah explains why he fled and when God explains why he forced him to prophesy and why he did not punish Nineveh.

7. The Purpose of the Book

The purpose of the story is to set forth a moral problem and suggest a solution. Kaufmann believes that in the earliest part of the Old Testament there is no room for repentance. Sin is simply punished. The generations of the flood and the Tower of Babel, the people of Sodom and the Canaanites are not called upon to repent. Even in the story of David's remorse after adultery, punishment follows (2 Sam. 12.13-15). However, in Jonah, Israel's developed concept of repentance, where the change of heart and its reflection in deed is the core of atonement, comes to the fore. Jonah is outraged when Nineveh repents and God annuls his decree, not because he is a narrow-minded zealot but because he is a champion of divine justice. He represents the ancient voice that sin must be punished. This view is challenged by the author in ch. 4. A change of heart and corresponding action are themselves capable of atoning for sin.

Kaufmann has some difficulty with the foreign setting of the story. After all, if the message has nothing to do with the Gentiles why involve them at all? His reply to this question would be that the author wants to give maximum play to his conception of the power of repentance. The Ninevites might resort to priests, temples, magic and sacrifice to expiate their sin, but they do not! They repent, and that repentance suffices to secure the forgiveness of God (3.10).

Clements takes a view not dissimilar to that of Kaufmann. Rejecting the universalistic interpretation, he points out that the interest in the book is entirely taken up with Jonah's own reaction to what has happened and its meaning for his work as a prophet. The story demonstrates the possibility of a change of heart both for human beings and for God. Since repentance is a possibility for humans it is also a possibility for God. Jonah is not angry that the beneficiaries of God's change of plan are Ninevites—this is not even hinted at—but that the divine plan has been changed at all. His concern is that his message is not fulfilled. That is why the events relating to his call and flight are an essential part of the story (Clements argues that the 'universalists' do not need the earlier part of the story at all). The events of ch. 1 emphasize that Jonah's call was real, that Yahweh was behind the call, the storm, the fish and the rescue, and, above all, the message which was delivered. And yet, although there was an announcement of doom a disaster did not happen. The conclusion is that when God passes a sentence of death he leaves open a way of escape, that is, repentance. The author is concerned that Israel should see this as a possibility.

Why would the author need to make such a statement? Clements draws attention to the fact that in early prophecy prophets announced what Yahweh was about to do and gave reasons for his actions. Occasionally they might appeal to their audience to return to Yahweh but they were unsure of the consequence of such action. But when we come to the sixth century we find that repentance has become more prominent. In Jeremiah (18.11; 25.5; 26.3; 29.10-14; 36; 37), in the Deuteronomistic history, in Ezekiel (18.1-3), and in the editing of the pre-exilic prophets there is a growing concern with the theme of repentance. The disaster announced by God through the prophets may have come to pass, but Israel was not utterly blotted out. The presentation of these threats with the appended words of hope indicated that all was not lost for Israel, and together they served as an appeal to the people to recognize God's ways and to return to him.

Perhaps one reason why Clements too has not had a great following for his interpretation is to be found in his treatment of the setting of the story. The dispute which Jonah has with God takes place in Nineveh; there is nothing remotely comparable with this in the other prophetic books. Yet Clements dismisses this as incidental: 'It is simply a feature belonging to the chosen setting of the story that the people threatened should be Ninevites, for it makes no difference to the point that is being made whatever race or religion they belong to'. Not a few scholars find this attitude to 'mission to Nineveh' unsatisfactory. To ignore this feature as Clements seems to do is to disregard the background to Jonah's audience or readership. What would be the reaction of ancient Israelites or Jews to the Ninevites? Is it possible that they would not have noticed this feature or would have regarded the target of Jonah's preaching in much the same way as if it had been the city of Megiddo? It is not enough to observe that the Ninevites

7. The Purpose of the Book

are not presented as the arch-enemies of Israel. We may perhaps compare the New Testament parable of the Good Samaritan (Lk. 10.30-37). There is nothing in that story to suggest Jewish–Samaritan conflict, but it would be a bold and foolish commentator on Luke's Gospel who would ignore these issues in interpreting the passage.

The key to understanding the intention of the author of Jonah is surely to be found in ch. 4, in the discussion between God and Jonah, and in the context of pagan Nineveh. That is not to say that the previous chapters do not serve any purpose other than preamble. On the contrary, ch. 1 points up the belief that Yahweh, the God of heaven, is the maker of earth and sea, and is in control of the elements and his creatures; it also points out that God's will is fulfilled in spite of disobedience on the part of his servant: his will cannot be resisted; and it emphasizes the divine origin of Jonah's message of doom.

Whether the psalm of ch. 2 is original or not does not affect the message of the book as a whole. As it stands the psalm is a song of thanksgiving for deliverance on the part of Jonah, and, as such, adds emphasis to the idea of divine control. Chapter 3 has to do with Jonah's successful mission to Nineveh. One should not deduce from this success any homiletical lessons, or conclude that Jonah was a greater preacher than, say, Jeremiah! The emphasis here is on the completeness of the repentance and on God's change of heart towards the Ninevites.

It is here, at the beginning of ch. 4, that the reason for Jonah's reluctance begins to become clear; and it is at the end of this chapter that we come to the essence of the problem. Jonah is angry that God has not carried out the threat pronounced. There is no allusion to the Gentiles here, no reference to the hated Ninevites, no hint at God's special relationship to Israel; but there is a reference to God's mercy and to his readiness to change his mind: 'I knew that thou art a gracious God and merciful, slow to anger, and abounding in steadfast love, and repentest of evil' (Jon. 4.2b). And there is the implication that Jonah was not in agreement or could not cope with the divine change of mind. Does Jonah represent a view, discarded by our author but prevalent in his time, that a message of God was bound to be fulfilled, or that if a prophet made a pronouncement his credentials would be in tatters if that pronouncement were not to be fulfilled? Such a view is based on Deut. 18.21-22:

> And if you say in your heart, 'How may we know the word which the Lord has not spoken?' When a prophet speaks in the name of the Lord, if the word does not come to pass or come true, that is a word which the Lord has not spoken; the prophet has spoken it presumptuously; you need not be afraid of him.

This passage makes it clear that a prophet whose words are not fulfilled should be disregarded, that his message is not from God; and yet the author of Jonah is at pains to emphasize that Jonah's commission and message were authentic. It is clear that our author believed in God's freedom to change his mind; and he may have had a further passage in mind here, Jer. 18.7-8:

> If at any time I declare concerning a nation or a kingdom, that I will pluck up and break down and destroy it, and if that nation, concerning which I have spoken, turns from its evil, I will repent of the evil that I intended to do to it.

But creation theology underlies the argument that follows (Jon. 4.2b). God may be free to 'repent', but the target of his mercy is his creation. No mention is made of covenant; and the absence of the name 'Israel' together with the presence of the name 'Nineveh' is very significant. God is free to change his mind, free to have mercy on all who repent, even the hated and evil Ninevites, who are his creatures.

The purpose of the book, then, is not a simple one. The author wishes to stress that even an authentic pronouncement of doom by a genuine prophet of God may not be fulfilled. Repentance may provide a way of escape. For the divine heart is full of mercy and extends to all his creatures, even to those whom we are wont to despise. The debate will nonetheless continue. One group of scholars will emphasize one aspect of the book while another will find quite another interpretation by fixing on another aspect of the story.

7. The Purpose of the Book

Further Reading

The student should, perhaps, concentrate at first on the work by E. Bickerman, *Four Strange Books of the Bible* (New York: Schocken Books, 1967), pp. 1-49, which gives a flavour of the history of the book's interpretation. A fuller, and annotated, version of this appeared as 'Les deux erreurs du prophète Jonas', *RHPR* 45 (1965), pp. 232-64.

A fine survey of early thinking on Jonah is to be found in Y.-M. Duval, *Le livre de Jonas dans la littérature chrétienne grecque et latine* (Paris: Etudes augustiniennes, 1973).

A sample of mediaeval Jewish thinking can be found in A.J. Rosenberg, *The Book of the Twelve Prophets (A New English Translation of the Text, Rashi, and a Commentary Digest)*, I (New York: Judaica Press, 1986).

The Reformation is represented in H.C. Oswald (ed.), *Lectures on the Minor Prophets II (Luther's Works 19)* (St Louis, MO: Concordia, 1974); and in J. Owen (ed.), *Commentaries on the Twelve Minor Prophets by John Calvin*, III (Edinburgh: Calvin Translation Society, 1847).

Later Views

R.E. Clements, 'The Purpose of the Book of Jonah', in J.A. Emerton *et al.* (eds.), *Congress Volume Edinburgh 1974* (VTSup, 28; Leiden: Brill, 1975), pp. 16-28.

D. Daube, 'Jonah: A Reminiscence', *JJS* 35 (1984), pp. 36-43.

Day, 'Problems in the Interpretation of the Book of Jonah', pp. 44-47.

G. Fohrer, *Introduction to the Old Testament* (London: SPCK, 1968).

H. Gevaryahu, 'The Universalism of the Book of Jonah', *Dor le Dor* 10 (1981), pp. 20-27.

G.I. Emmerson, 'Another Look at the Book of Jonah', *ExpTim* 88 (1976), pp. 86-87.

Feuillet, 'Le sens du livre Jonas', pp. 340-61.

Fretheim, *The Message of Jonah*.

S.D.F. Goitein, 'Some Observations on Jonah', *JPOS* 17 (1937), pp. 71-73.

Golka, *The Song of Songs and Jonah*.

F. Hitzig, *Die zwölf kleinen Propheten* (Leipzig: S. Hirzel, 1881), p. 174.

Y. Kaufmann, *The Religion of Israel* (Chicago: University of Chicago Press, 1961).

E. Nielsen, 'Le message primitif du livre de Jonas', *RHPR* 59 (1979), pp. 499-507.

D.F. Payne, 'Jonah from the Perspective of its Audience', *JSOT* 13 (1979), pp. 3-12.

H.H. Rowley, *The Missionary Message of the Old Testament* (London: Carey Press, 1945).
Rudolph, *Jona*.
Sasson, *Jonah*.
Wolff, *Obadiah and Jonah*.

Part II

LAMENTATIONS

Select List of Commentaries

R. Davidson, *Jeremiah Vol II and Lamentations* (DSB; Edinburgh: St Andrew Press; Philadelphia: Westminster Press, 1985). This is not a detailed commentary but it is perceptive and useful.

W.J. Fuerst, *The Books of Ruth, Esther, Ecclesiastes, The Song of Songs, Lamentations* (CNEB; Cambridge: Cambridge University Press, 1975), pp. 201-64. Based on the text of the NEB, this is a good basic commentary which provides a fair section on the historical background.

R. Gordis, *The Song of Songs and Lamentations* (New York: Ktav, rev. edn, 1974). Anything by Gordis is worth consulting, although the student requires Hebrew in order to understand it fully.

A.S. Herbert, 'Lamentations', in Black and Rowley (eds.), *Peake's Commentary on the Bible*, pp. 563-67. A fairly short commentary but sensitively written.

D.R. Hillers, *Lamentations* (AB, 7a; Garden City, NY: Doubleday, 2nd edn, 1992). This is the best commentary in English. The student requires Hebrew for the Notes section, but the Comment (after each chapter), which is very valuable, is accessible to the non-Hebraist.

T.J. Meek, 'The Book of Lamentations', *IB*, VI (Nashville: Abingdon Press, 1956), pp. 1-38. This is a commentary worth consulting. Hebrew is a help but not essential.

C.W.E. Nägelsbach, *The Lamentations of Jeremiah* (ed. and trans. W.H. Hornblower; New York: Scribner, 1871). This is dated but well worth consulting. The editor disagrees with Nägelsbach and often intrudes.

I.W. Provan, *Lamentations* (NCB; London: Marshall, Morgan & Scott; Grand Rapids: Eerdmans, 1991). One of the better commentaries. The author disagrees with the usual tendency to interpret specifically in the light of the Fall of Jerusalem.

S.P. Re'emi, *God's People in Crisis: A Commentary on the Book of Amos; A Commentary on the Book of Lamentations* (ITC; Edinburgh: Handsel Press; Grand Rapids: Eerdmans, 1984), pp. 73-134. This is a short but carefully written commentary with theological leanings.

A.W. Streane, *Jeremiah, Lamentations* (CBS; Cambridge: Cambridge University Press, 1926), pp. 353-91. Short and a little dated.

Foreign-language commentaries

H.-J. Kraus, *Klagelieder* (BKAT, 20; Neukirchen–Vluyn: Neukirchener Verlag, 3rd edn, 1968). Fairly concise commentary.

W. Rudolph, *Das Buch Ruth—Das Hohe Lied—Die Klagelieder* (KAT, 17.1-3; Gütersloh: Gerd Mohn, 1962). In addition to a translation and detailed notes, there is a commentary on each chapter; but the student will require Hebrew for an adequate understanding.

C. Westermann, *Die Klagelieder: Forschungsgeschichte und Auslegung* (Neukirchen–Vluyn: Neukirchener Verlag, 1990). Concise, but very informative. Before the commentary on the text there is a section on the question of genre—where the views of Jahnow, Kraus and McDaniel are discussed—and a useful section on the history of interpretation 1920–1985.

Two works which are not commentaries as such but are very important for the study of Lamentations are:

B. Albrektson, *Studies in the Text and Theology of the Book of Lamentations* (Studia Theologica Lundensia, 21; Lund: Gleerup, 1963). While the student requires Hebrew, Greek and Syriac to follow this study, the final section, pp. 214-39, on the theology of the book, is accessible to the non-linguist.

N.K. Gottwald, *Studies in the Book of Lamentations* (SBT, 14; London: SCM Press, 1962). This is a must for any study of Lamentations.

1
INTRODUCTION

IN THE FIELD OF OLD TESTAMENT study the book of Lamentations is a neglected book. That it has probably always been neglected is evident from the dearth of attention that it has received in the history of biblical interpretation. Why should this be so? Is it because it is a small book? If that were the reason we should expect Jonah, Micah or Ruth to have suffered the same fate; but this is not the case. Could it be that its name and its theme have been against it, that students of the Old Testament did not wish to dwell on doom and gloom, a theme to which the book of Lamentations is thought to be devoted? There may be something in this suggestion, although one could point out that the book of Job also has to do with suffering, pain and gloom, and yet has been the focus of much study. Job is however very different from Lamentations in that it is mostly a debate on the question of the suffering of the innocent; furthermore, the debate is set in the context of a story, and there is a happy ending! It is possible, then, that the fact that the book of Lamentations consists of five almost unrelieved laments has been a factor in its neglect.

Another possible reason is the fact that it has long been thought to have been written by the prophet Jeremiah; and since there are laments within the book of Jeremiah, attention has been concentrated on the book proper, and the prophecy proper. That is to say, Lamentations may have been considered peripheral to Jeremiah studies, and even more peripheral to Old Testament study. But during this century the majority of scholars have tended to question the link with

Jeremiah, and it is during this century that interest in Lamentations has begun to increase. But while the study of the book may have been neglected by biblical scholars, it has, like the Psalms, with which it has affinities, caught the imagination of those in the arts and, especially, of musicians. J.H. Tigay draws attention to an epic poem *Treny* written in 1580 by Jan Kochanowski, a Polish writer. In 1613 the Spanish writer F. Gomez de Quevedo y Villegos wrote *Lagrimas de Hieremias castellanas*, and in 1752 was published the poem *Les lamentations de Jérémie* by F.-T. de Baculard d'Arnaud. In the field of music composition Lamentations was especially popular in the sixteenth century, perhaps the most notable compositions being the settings of Tallis, Byrd, Viadana and Rosenmueller. We also have Bach's Cantata 46, *Schauet doch und sehet*. More recent are the notable *Jeremiah Symphony* by Leonard Bernstein (1943) in which the Hebrew text of the first chapter of Lamentations is sung by a mezzo-soprano, and Igor Stravinsky's *Threni, id est Lamentationes Jeremiae prophetae*, which was first performed in 1958.

The Name of the Book

The name in English translations—Lamentations—comes to us via the Vulgate, *Lamentationes*; this, in turn, appears to be a translation of the Greek *threnoi* in the Septuagint. It is a descriptive title. Pfeiffer thinks that it is a translation of the Hebrew *qînôt* which appears as the book's title in the Babylonian Talmud (*b. B. Bat.* 14b), and in transliterated form in Jerome's *Prologus Galeatus* (*cinoth*). However, it may be that the Septuagint title was given to it by the Greek translator, and that thereafter the book was sometimes referred to by this name or by a translation of it (into Hebrew). The book has no title as such in the Hebrew Bible, and in Jewish circles it is more often than not alluded to by the book's opening word *'êkâ* (just as the first book, which we call Genesis, is referred to by its first word *b^{e}rē'šît*).

1. *Introduction*

Place in the Canon

Unlike some other members of the Megillot—Ecclesiastes, Song of Songs and Esther—the canonical status of the book of Lamentations has never been called in question; at least, there is no record of doubts about its status. This may be because it became so closely associated with the prophet Jeremiah that it was not viewed as a separate entity. Indeed, although Jerome notes that in some circles the book is to be found among the Hagiographa or Writings (the third section of the Hebrew Scriptures, the other two being Law and Prophets), he himself views it as part of the book of Jeremiah; and Josephus treats the two books as one in his enumeration of holy books (cf. Hillers). As has already been mentioned, Lamentations stands after Jeremiah in the Septuagint, and it is that placing which carried over via the Vulgate into the Authorised Version and most modern translations.

The exceptions are the Jewish translations (cf. NJV) whose translators follow the Hebrew grouping. In the Hebrew tradition Lamentations is found not in the Prophets but in the Writings; however, within that section its position varies. For example, the Babylonian Talmud, in a passage which appears to deal with chronological order (although Barton wonders if this is so) states: 'the order of the writings is Ruth, Psalms, Job, Proverbs, Ecclesiastes, Song of Songs, Lamentations, Daniel, Esther, Ezra and Chronicles' (*b. B. Bat.* 14b). There the five scrolls (the Megillot) are not placed together but scattered throughout the section, and Lamentations comes well down the list. But elsewhere, in editions of the Hebrew Bible and in manuscripts, books are grouped according to Jewish liturgical practice. The books known as the five scrolls, which were linked traditionally with the five major Jewish festivals, are there grouped together. But there also was no fixed tradition. Wolfenson has shown that even in printed Jewish Bibles there was no uniformity in grouping the books; occasionally we find the Megillot between the Torah (Law) and the Prophets, while at other times each of the five Megillot has been inserted after a book of the Torah. These practices presumably reflect liturgical interests. In Jewish tradition, these five books belong to the section of the Hebrew Bible known as the Writings (*kᵉtûbîm*), although the order in which they appear also varies. In some manuscripts and printed Bibles the order seems to be controlled by the order in which the great Jewish festivals occur. Hence there is a strong tradition which runs: Song of Songs (Passover), Ruth (Weeks), Lamentations (Ninth of Ab), Ecclesiastes (Sukkot), Esther (Purim).

The modern editions of the Hebrew Bible (for instance *BHK*, *BHS*) follow more or less the order of the eleventh-century manuscript the Codex Leningradensis. This lists the Megillot in what was thought to be a chronological order: Ruth, Song of Songs (the young Solomon), Ecclesiastes (the old Solomon), Lamentations and Esther. There is, therefore, no 'correct' or original order. Indeed, although we may make observations as to the place Lamentations finds itself in one or other codex, the idea of order was probably meaningless in the pre-codex era when works existed as separate scrolls.

Liturgical Use

It is impossible to know if these poems were used for worship services at a very early period. It is possible that they were composed precisely for liturgical use; it is also possible that they were collected together for that use although written with another purpose in mind. Gottwald thinks that the poems were in use regularly throughout the exile (commemorating the fall of Jerusalem) and perhaps thereafter on select occasions. He may be jumping to conclusions here, for the evidence is thin, and his observation that phrases in the poems were known 'to the cultic-minded Chronicler (see 2 Chron. 36.16-19) is not strong support for his argument.

It is likely, however, that these poems, once written (for whatever reason), would have 'commemorated' the destruction of the city and the Temple for those who read them, and it is a small step from this to their use in a public ceremony. If we compare the poems with the laments in the book of Psalms we might make the deduction that this kind of literature, used

1. *Introduction* 71

in Judaism in the Second Temple period for public worship, would be utilized for the same ends. As Hillers says,

> Nothing in the poems precludes such a use. Although some scholars have raised doubts on this point, common readers with some experience in public worship may well trust their own judgment on this point. Formal characteristics, such as the use of 'I' in many passages, do not rule out the idea that they were written, or at least soon used, in corporate worship, nor does the use of acrostic form compel us to think that chapters 1–4 were intended only for private study and devotion.

The fact that the poems draw on the lament tradition in Israel and that they contain the ingredients of petition, confession and imprecation is another factor pointing to the conclusion that they may have served the purpose of public worship.

Another pointer may be Zech. 7.3-5, which refers to mourning and fasting in the fifth month (Ab), implying that this had been customary for the previous seventy years. In later Jewish practice the book of Lamentations was, on the ninth of Ab, associated with the commemoration of the fall of Jerusalem in 586 BCE and 70 CE; and this custom may go back a long way.

The Christian church, searching the Scriptures for references to Jesus, fixed on a number of passages in Lamentations which, it was felt, pointed to Christ. Phrases like 'the Lord's anointed' (4.20) and 'let him give his cheek to the smiter' (3.30) were thought to be clear allusions to Jesus; and the agony on the cross was thought to have been prefigured at 1.12: 'Is it nothing to you, all you who pass by? Look and see if there is any sorrow like my sorrow which was brought upon me, which the Lord inflicted on the day of his fierce anger' (cf. the later use made of this passage in Bach's Cantata 46, and in Handel's *Messiah*). But even where the text did not 'refer' to Christ, words from Lamentations were used in Christian liturgical services, in particular in the *Tenebrae*, the Matins–Lauds Services for the final days of Holy Week, where Lam. 1.1-5 was the passage set to music.

Further Reading

J. Barr, *Holy Scripture* (Oxford: Oxford University Press, 1983).

J. Barton, *Oracles of God: Perceptions of Ancient Prophecy in Israel after the Exile* (London: Darton, Longman & Todd, 1986), especially chapter 2.

O. Eissfeldt, *The Old Testament: An Introduction* (Oxford: Basil Blackwell, 1965).

Gottwald, *Studies in the Book of Lamentations*, pp. 113-14.

Hillers, *Lamentations*, pp. 6ff.

Jerome, *Patrologia Latina* 28.593-604.

Josephus, *Apion* 1.8.

R.H. Pfeiffer, *Introduction to the Old Testament* (London and New York: Harper & Brothers, 1941).

Provan, *Lamentations*, pp. 3-4.

J.H. Tigay, 'Lamentations', *EncJud*, X, pp. 1368-75.

L.B. Wolfenson, 'Implications of the Place of Ruth in Editions, Manuscripts, and Canon of the Old Testament', *HUCA* 1 (1924), pp. 151-78.

For an example of a sixteenth-century setting of Lam. 1.1-5 by Thomas Tallis, see *Thomas Tallis: The Lamentations of Jeremiah* (ed. P. Brett; London: Oxford University Press, 1967).

2

OUTLINE
OF THE BOOK

Chapter 1

THE AUTHOR LAMENTS the desolation of the city of Jerusalem. Her (the city is personified as female) inhabitants have gone into exile; her invaders have seized her valuable goods and treasures; her glory has gone (1.1-11a).

The personified city speaks, describing the agony she feels, and making clear that it is Yahweh who is the author of her affliction—a just and due punishment for her transgressions. At the same time she calls for retribution on her gloating enemies. This section, in the first person, is interrupted by a verse (17) in the third person which is on the same lines as vv. 1-11a, describing the plight of Jerusalem (1.11b-22).

Chapter 2

The author here concentrates on the *cause* of the affliction. This was Yahweh's anger. It was he who had destroyed the people, wrecked their stronghold, dethroned their rulers and withdrawn his support. In fact, Yahweh has become the enemy of his people, his land, his sanctuary; he has caused the exile of the king and princes and has broken off communication with the prophets (2.1-9).

Those left behind in Jerusalem are in mourning; they are destitute and suffer famine. Those who travel past Jerusalem mock; their enemies gloat over the destruction (2.10-17).

The poet calls on Jerusalem to cry out to Yahweh with tears, in sincerity and without ceasing (2.18-19).

The personified city then prays to Yahweh, alluding to the distress of famine, the slaughter of the religious leaders and the youth (2.20-22).

Chapter 3

In this poem the speaker begins in a lament to describe his own experience of the affliction already alluded to. He is despised as a result of Yahweh's activity (3.1-18).

There follows a prayer and a statement of trust (3.19-24). These are followed by a discussion of the significance of suffering in which the speaker deals with the views of the sceptic who may doubt that Yahweh is really in control (3.25-39).

The speaker now calls upon others to repent (3.40-42). This call is followed by renewed lament, although the subject matter is now the suffering of others at the hand of Yahweh (3.43-51).

Finally, there is a return to the theme of the speaker's individual suffering, in particular suffering inflicted not by Yahweh but by the enemies. The speaker calls on Yahweh for help, and the final verses are given over to a confident appeal to Yahweh for vengeance on the enemy (3.52-66).

Chapter 4

Here the author describes the ghastly experiences in the streets of Jerusalem—famine and drought—and contrasts the present with the past. The lucky ones were those who were killed by the sword (4.1-11).

The plight of priests and prophets is now given attention. They had been the main culprits, and now their state is such that they are unclean even in the eyes of the heathen (4.12-16).

There is an allusion to an expectation of help from Egypt which ended in disappointment (4.17), and a reference to the flight of the king from Jerusalem which ended in failure (4.18-20).

Finally, although Edom may rejoice for a while, there is a time coming when Jerusalem's punishment will be at an end, and it will be Edom's turn to suffer (4.21-22).

Chapter 5

The final poem calls on Yahweh to consider the affliction of his people: lands and homes in the hands of aliens, women raped throughout the land, occupied Judah a dangerous and rough place to live (5.1-18). The final verses are a prayer to Yahweh for restoration (5.19-22).

3
HISTORICAL BACKGROUND

Identifying the Period

It is notoriously difficult to date psalms whether of lament or of thanksgiving. In the Old Testament book of Psalms there are very few (perhaps Pss. 74 and 79, but not many others) which allow us to link the contents with other known events in the life of the communities of Israel and Judah. The sentiments expressed and the contents are such that one might apply them to any of several aspects or moments in the history of the people who produced them. This may be because the collectors of the psalms strove to provide a collection which could be used in temple or synagogue on a variety of occasions and applied to a variety of situations. Thus a psalm of thanksgiving which was composed on the occasion of a particular community's deliverance from a particular enemy might be utilized thereafter to lift the hearts of a community after another deliverance from yet another enemy, and long after the original generation had ceased to exist.

The linking of the name of David with the book of Psalms led eventually to the question 'of what was David thinking when he composed such and such a psalm?', and the answers are reflected to some extent in the titles of some psalms: for example, the rubric of Psalm 51 reads '...*Psalm of David. When Nathan the Prophet came to him, after he had gone in to Bathsheba*'. A considerable amount of guesswork went into those 'historical' titles (cf. Anderson), and many scholars tend to regard them sceptically, so much so that the NEB (1970) translators omitted them altogether, though this has been reversed in the REB (1989).

3. Historical Background

The five poems which comprise the book of Lamentations are similar to some of the literature included in the book of Psalms. None of them has a superscription, and the book itself has no editorial beginning as do for example Isaiah, Jeremiah, Hosea and Amos. The Greek version of Lamentations does have a superscription which links the poems to Jeremiah and to the period just after the destruction of Jerusalem in 586 BCE (see the section below on authorship) when large numbers of the people had gone into captivity. While not a few scholars are sceptical about the link with Jeremiah, most commentators argue that the poems were written after 586 BCE and perhaps not long after that date, although a few (for instance Rudolph) hold that ch. 1 was written shortly after 597 BCE. The evidence, perhaps suggested by the Septuagint superscription, is usually adduced from the allusions in the poems themselves, although these poems provide few specific references. At 4.17 we read, 'We watched for a nation which could not save', and this is usually thought to refer to Egypt (though see Provan, who thinks it could refer to Edom); and at 4.20 'The Lord's anointed' is often taken to be Zedekiah, who was king in 586 BCE, although no name is given in the text. The names Assyria and Egypt (5.6) and Edom (4.21-22) are mentioned, but the references are too vague to tie the respective passages to any particular historical event. Hence, on a formal level, the book of Lamentations appears to be very loosely connected to history; and Provan will go no further than to admit that troubled times have given rise to these poems.

There are, however, some indications that we are in fact dealing with a specific period in Israel's history. To begin with, there are many references to the devastation of Jerusalem or Zion (2.5; 5.18), references to exile (1.3), to the end of the kingdom and its rulers (2.6), to the destruction of the temple (2.6), to famine (2.12), to the invasion of Jerusalem (4.12). While it could be argued that the author might have employed hyperbole to describe a severe setback or hardship, some statements cannot be so interpreted; for instance 1.3, 'Judah has gone into exile because of affliction; she dwells now among the nations'; 2.6, 'He has broken down his booth like that of a garden, laid in ruins the place of his appointed feasts'; 4.12, 'The kings of the earth did not believe, or any inhabitants of the world, that foe or enemy could enter the gates of Jerusalem'. These texts refer to the captivity, the destruction of the temple and the end of the belief in the inviolability of Jerusalem; and they can surely only have arisen from the events of the early sixth century BCE, It may be argued that the five poems are all of different origin—that is, not necessarily by one author or from the same time—and that each may be alluding to a different period; but, while the character of ch. 3 is not easy to explain, the impression given is that we are in the sixth century BCE. Rudolph has argued that ch. 1 refers to the Babylonian invasion of 597 BCE, to the capture of Jerusalem only, and not to its destruction. While this is a possibility, most scholars are unconvinced, and feel that the language of this chapter is too extreme to refer to the period 597–589 BCE. It seems clear that we are in a period when Judah and Jerusalem have been devastated, surely the final death throes of the kingdom of Judah. It is, of course, possible that the books of Kings and Chronicles do not recall all the hardships and invasions suffered by the people of the Old Testament, and we have to acknowledge that our identification of the calamities referred to in Lamentations is dependent to some extent on information from other parts of the Old Testament.

The Background

The fall of Jerusalem with the destruction of the state of Judah in 586 BCE was a watershed in the history of the people. Apart from the loss of statehood, the exile of the skilled and the nobility and the devastation of the countryside and the cities of Judah, it was the destruction of the capital city, and especially of the temple, which had the greatest impact. The prophet Jeremiah had encountered the view that because Yahweh dwelt in the Jerusalem temple the city could not be captured; and those who held this view—influential people—considered Jeremiah a faithless traitor when he stated that all would be laid waste (cf. Jer. 7.1-20; 26). This strongly held

3. Historical Background

view was now in tatters, and with it faith in Yahweh was severely tested, with the people wondering whether Yahweh was capable of protecting them. Furthermore, the whole system of Yahweh worship—the sacrificial system and the festivals— had ceased with the temple's destruction. With the leaders in Babylonia, those left behind in Judah were stunned.

The countdown to the fall of Judah probably began with the demise of the Assyrian empire in 612 BCE. Before that (although in decline since 639 BCE), Assyria had created a massive empire which included Syria-Palestine and had involved the annihilation of Judah's neighbour Israel; and the kings of Judah had consequently been anxious not to offend in case they were singled out for attention. But long before the fall of the Assyrian capital Nineveh in 612 BCE, the power of the great empire had been on the wane, and Judah, for one, hoped for relief from the overlord. King Josiah of Judah (639–609 BCE) may well have had ambitions of restoring to the people of Yahweh the old lands and borders of the Solomonic kingdom. In any event he appears to have pushed his borders outwards and, at least, northwards (see Malamat, 'The Last Kings') by the time of his death in 609 BCE at the hands of Pharaoh Necho of Egypt who, in the power vacuum created by the fall of Assyria, had also seen his chance of gain (2 Kgs 23.28-30; cf. 2 Chron. 35.20-26).

Shortly after this, Necho laid claim to Syria-Palestine. Jehoahaz, who had taken the throne in succession to his father Josiah, was removed by Necho, who then placed Jehoahaz's elder brother, Eliakim on the throne. In doing so, Necho changed Eliakim's name to Jehoiakim, thereby demonstrating his (Necho's) authority in Judah.

With the demise of Assyria, a power struggle ensued. The Babylonians and the Medes had been instrumental in this overthrow and began to divide the Assyrian empire between them. The Medes took control of most of Assyria proper plus the hill country to the north, while the Babylonians took over the rest of Mesopotamia and, having defeated the final Assyrian resistance (supported by Necho) at Haran in 609 BCE, laid claim to Syria and Palestine. This claim was bound to be challenged by Egypt, and in 605 BCE Babylon and Egypt met in battle at Carchemish (Jer. 46). According to Babylonian sources (cf. Wiseman) and Jeremiah, the Egyptian army was routed by Nebuchadnezzar, the crown prince, and Necho had to yield Syria and Palestine. (According to 2 Kgs 24.7 Necho was confined to his own land thereafter.) With these changes of control, the smaller states in Syria and Palestine sought to make the most of the situation, and Nebuchadnezzar was kept busy in the area, conducting several campaigns over the next few years. The Babylonian king then tried to invade Egypt (601 BCE) but was defeated by the Egyptian army and returned to Babylon. It is at this point of Babylonian weakness that Jehoiakim rebelled against Nebuchadnezzar (2 Kgs 24.1). Two years later, Nebuchadnezzar again marched west, and then again in 598 BCE, this time with Jerusalem and Jehoiakim in mind. He laid siege to Jerusalem, and the city fell in 597 BCE, although Jehoiakim had died in the meantime and Jehoiachin had succeeded his father. In order to assert his authority Nebuchadnezzar removed Jehoiachin from the throne, took him into exile in Babylon and placed his uncle, Mataniah, on the throne, changing his name to Zedekiah.

The fall of Jerusalem in 597 BCE was a surrender. The city was not destroyed, but a heavy tribute was paid to Babylon and the Temple was plundered. More importantly, the king, his mother, his wives and his officials were taken to Babylon, along with many skilled and influential people, not only from Jerusalem but also from Judah. Zedekiah was required to make a treaty of vassalage with Nebuchadnezzar (2 Chron 36.13-14; Ezek. 17.12-14) the breaking of which would have severe consequences for Judah.

Not much is known about the period 597–589 BCE although we may conclude that with so many important figures (not to mention artisans and working people) taken into exile there would have been considerable upheaval in the administration of the country and the city, and the quality of life under Zedekiah cannot have been high. The books of Jeremiah and Ezekiel are important here. Jeremiah advised the people and the king to accept the Babylonian yoke as the only way to survive (Jer. 27.12). Ezekiel, a deportee in 597 BCE, challenged

3. Historical Background 81

the view, prevalent among the exiles, that the captivity was provisional and that the exiles would soon return to Judah. The Old Testament baldly states (2 Kgs 25.1) that Zedekiah rebelled against the king of Babylon; in view of the circumstances this appears to have been madness on his part. But Zedekiah would not have rebelled without some indication, however misinterpreted, that his rebellion might be successful. Apart from some unrest in Phoenicia, there is evidence that Egypt was on the move, and the king of Egypt may have instigated a rebellion among states in the area. In any case Zedekiah broke with Nebuchadnezzar (see Malamat, 'The Last Kings'; cf. Ezek. 17.15), and Nebuchadnezzar sent his army to besiege Jerusalem, which held out for about two years. Egyptian help was absent and only arrived after the siege was about a year old (Ezek. 29.1-16; 30.20-26; 31.1-18, and see Malamat, 'The Last Kings'). The Babylonian army withdrew temporarily to deal with this threat, but then resumed the siege and tightened the grip on the city. In 586 BCE, when the people of Jerusalem must have been in dire straits, a breach was made in the city walls; and Zedekiah and his entourage escaped by night and fled towards the Jordan valley. But the Babylonians overtook him and he was brutally treated by Nebuchadnezzar and taken to Babylon (for his last days see 2 Kgs 25). We may assume—and this is confirmed by archaeological excavations—that most communities in Judah had already been devastated by the Babylonian army. The city of Jerusalem was largely destroyed, including the temple.

Part of the population was taken in captivity to Babylon (Jer. 52.28-30 says 832 were taken at that time) and, according to 2 Kings, only the peasants were allowed to remain. Unlike the Assyrians, who deported much of the population and replaced it with deportees from other parts of the empire, the Babylonians did not, it seems, transplant a foreign nobility to Jerusalem. In fact, they appointed Gedaliah, a local Judahite, as governor of what appears to have been a Babylonian province, although the word 'province' is never mentioned. But the situation did not settle down immediately. Gedaliah was murdered by a certain Ishmael (of Davidic blood) and others, who probably considered that Gedaliah had 'sold out' to the Babylonians. Instigated by the king of Ammon and others, they were hoping for an overthrow of the Babylonian overlord. Many fled the country, although Jeremiah advised against it, one group at least going to Egypt, taking Jeremiah with them. Jeremiah (52.30) refers to another deportation (745 people) in 582 BCE which may have been the result of Babylonian reprisals.

The impression we get from reading the biblical texts and the Babylonian annals is that the whole country had been devastated, that the population had been reduced through captivity and voluntary exile, as well as death by the sword and through famine. This is also the impression given by archaeological excavations which show that there was a total destruction of most towns in the area.

Judah's neighbours, Edom, Ammon and Moab, were still in existence at 586 BCE and do not seem to have been affected by this campaign. Furthermore, Jer. 40.11 states that at the fall of Jerusalem many Judahites fled to those countries, no doubt because they wished to escape the influence of the Babylonians. It may be that Ishmael's rebellion, aided and abetted by Ammon, was the result of intrigue amongst other states such as Edom and Moab, for Josephus tells us that in 582 BCE Nebuchadnezzar made war on Moab and Ammon and subjugated them, and this agrees with the further deportation of 582 people mentioned by Jeremiah (52.30). Edom may also have been involved here.

Further Reading

Y. Aharoni, *The Land of the Bible* (London: Burns & Oates, 2nd edn, 1979), pp. 400-407.
A.A. Anderson, *Psalms*, I (NCB: London: Oliphants, 1972), pp. 43-51.
J. Bright, *A History of Israel* (OTL; London: SCM Press, 1960), pp. 288-326.
S.B. Frost, 'The Death of Josiah: A Conspiracy of Silence', *JBL* 87 (1968), pp. 369-82.
Fuerst, *The Books of Ruth, Esther, Ecclesiastes, The Song of Songs, Lamentations*, pp. 201-205.
S. Herrmann, *The History of Israel in Old Testament Times* (London: SCM Press, 1975), pp. 263-85.

3. Historical Background

A. Malamat, 'The Last Kings of Judah and the Fall of Jerusalem', *IEJ* 18 (1968), pp. 137-55.
—'The Last Wars of the Kingdom of Judah', *JNES* 9 (1950), p. 218-27.
M. Noth, *The History of Israel* (London: A. & C. Black; 2nd edn, 1960), pp. 269-99.
—'The Jerusalem Catastrophe of 587 BCE and its Significance for Israel', in *The Laws in the Pentateuch and Other Studies* (Edinburgh and London: Oliver & Boyd, 1966), pp. 260-80.
B. Oded, 'Judah and the Exile', in J.H. Hayes and J.M. Miller (eds.), *Israelite and Judaean History* (OTL; London: SCM Press, 1977), pp. 435-88 (especially pp. 458-80).
J.A. Soggin, *A History of Israel* (London: SCM Press, 1984), pp. 231-57.
D.J. Wiseman, *Chronicles of the Chaldaean Kings (626–556 BCE) in the British Museum* (London: Trustees of the British Museum, 2nd edn, 1961).
—*People of Old Testament Times* (Oxford: Oxford University Press, 1973), chapters viii and x.

For arguments against the view that Lamentations was written in the light of the fall of Jerusalem in 586 BCE the student should consult:

I.W. Provan, 'Reading Texts against an Historical Background', *SJOT* 1 (1990), pp. 129-43.
—*Lamentations*, especially pp. 7-19.

4
THE POETRY OF LAMENTATIONS

Poetry in the Old Testament

EVEN A CURSORY GLANCE through the Old Testament, especially a version such as the RSV or NEB, is sufficient to notice that parts of it are set out in verse. Although the Authorized Version treated all parts of the text in a similar format, the Psalms and Proverbs have never really been thought of as being of the same genre as, say, Genesis. But the student may perhaps be surprised to find that much of the prophetic literature is set out in verse. The Old Testament writers were aware not only of the power of narrative, especially for historical writing, but also of the added impact that poetry and metaphor have always had on the human mind, and for this reason couched their thoughts in verse form and in poetic imagery.

Not a great deal is known about the technicalities of the poetry of ancient Israel. Indeed, scholars sometimes disagree as to the nature of the distinction between verse and prose in the Old Testament. A glance at the opening chapter of the book of Jeremiah in the RSV and NEB demonstrates this. Despite that, or perhaps because of that, quite a lot has been written on the subject. But while scholars on the whole are not yet in agreement, there are certain features of Hebrew verse which have been recognized by all scholars. Perhaps the chief of these characteristics is parallelism, a phenomenon observable in other ancient Near Eastern poetry—Egyptian, Canaanite, Akkadian and Aramaic (cf. Eissfeldt). It may be

4. The Poetry of Lamentations

described as the balancing of one half-line by the following one. There are three types of parallelism in the Old Testament.

1. A good example of the first is Ps. 34.1, 'I will bless the Lord at all times: His praise shall continually be in my mouth'. Here the second half parallels the first by expressing the same idea with different wording.
2. A variation of this is found when the second half parallel provides the *opposite* of the first; for example, 'A faithful witness does not lie, but a false witness breathes out lies' (Prov. 14.5).
3. A further variation is known as synthetic parallelism, where the second half takes the first half's idea further and completes it; for instance Ps. 2.6, 'I have set my king/on Zion, my holy hill'.

These three variations of parallelism are found frequently in Hebrew poetry.

What I have illustrated is parallelism of thoughts or ideas, but scholars have also noticed that the half-lines are balanced by their length or by the number of beats. Thus we find that there are often three beats to each half-line, occasionally two, occasionally four; and it is argued that originally this balance was the norm. In fact the balance is often broken; as well as 3:3, 4:4, 2:2 we find 3:4, 4:3, 3:2, 2:3 and so on. Indeed, as Watson observes, no single passage is written consistently in one style throughout. The need for tidiness has led some scholars to insist that originally the passages concerned were consistently of one or other rhythmic pattern; and there have not been wanting those who emend the text so as to 'restore' the lost consistency. But, as Watson remarks, we must accept the lack of regular metre as part and parcel of Hebrew verse tradition (see also Hillers).

Poetry in Lamentations

Although the Authorized Version makes no distinction in layout between verse and prose, it was always obvious that the language of Lamentations is poetic. The author is liberal in the use of metaphor and imagery; indeed, there is hardly a book in the Old Testament to rival Lamentations in this respect. The rhythm which predominates in Lamentations 1–4 is the 3:2 metre. Chapter 5 has the more familiar 3:3. Although the rhythm of chs. 1–4 may have been noticed earlier, it was K. Budde in 1882 who drew attention to the fact that in Lamentations the pattern 3:2 is clearly in the majority and argued that we ought to acknowledge this as the metrical pattern of the traditional Hebrew lament. He consequently entitled it the *qînâ* metre (the Hebrew for 'lament'). It is interesting to note that scholars have subsequently used the term *qînâ* to denote this metre although not all accept the whole of Budde's argument. Indeed, he may have exaggerated somewhat, for there are many lines in chs. 1–4, especially in ch. 1, which are not in the 3:2 pattern (for example 1.6a, 8a; 2.17c; 4.1a, 8b). Furthermore, the pattern is not confined either to Lamentations or to funeral songs or laments. Isa. 1.10-12; 40.9-11 and Song 1.9-11, for example, have this rhythm but are not laments by any stretch of the imagination. Again, the famous song by David about Saul and Jonathan (2 Sam. 1.17-27), clearly a lament, is not in this metre.

Budde's argument was that the lack of balance in the 3:2 metre conveyed itself to reader and hearer alike. Its very shape suggested that something was missing, that something was wrong, and that it had developed in the context of death and grief, where the mourners, in particular the professional and official mourners, wished to convey in word and action but also in the form of their verse (and no doubt in the style of their chants) that tragedy reigned. While translators cannot adequately convey the rhythm of the Hebrew metre, since it often takes more than one word to translate a Hebrew form, one may at times perceive the lack of balance, for example at 2.1:

> He has cast down from heaven to earth
> the splendour of Israel;
> he has not remembered his footstool
> in the day of his anger.

Here the unbalanced nature of the lines would be clear to hearers as well as to readers. If Budde is correct in his assertion that this 3:2 metre was originally associated with

4. The Poetry of Lamentations

lament, and if it was traditionally (although not always) used in lament, the form itself would be an important aspect of a lament and could convey an air of sadness even if the words were obscure.

Acrostics

Students using the English text of Lamentations in, say, the AV, RSV, or REB will probably be unaware that they are looking at alphabetic acrostics. This is because these versions conceal this phenomenon in their presentation. The AV shows inconsistency here; it sets out Psalm 119, an alphabetic acrostic, with the transliterated 22 letters of the Hebrew alphabet standing at the head of the 22 sections, while the existence of other acrostics (for example Ps. 34) is, as with Lamentations, not indicated; the result is that the phenomenon is hidden from view (although it is not clear even from the AV layout of Psalm 119 what the *purpose* of the Hebrew letters is). One reason for the omission may be that, in the Hebrew text of Lamentations itself, attention is not drawn to the feature, although it is highlighted in the case of Psalm 34 and other acrostic poems such as Psalms 25 and 119. The Septuagint carefully places the Hebrew letters *aleph*, *bet* and so on before the respective translated units; and the JB, which often takes note of the Greek, does the same. The student may get a flavour of the phenomenon by glancing at the translation of R.A. Knox, who reproduces it with English letters.

Readers of the Hebrew text of Lamentations (especially ch. 3) will, then, notice that the poems are closely related to the Hebrew alphabet. Each verse of chs. 1, 2 and 4 begins with a letter of the alphabet in sequence, while in ch. 3 each of the first *three* lines begins with *aleph*, the second three with *bet*, and so on. In ch. 5 there is a variation. This is not an acrostic, although it does contain 22 verses (the number of letters in the Hebrew alphabet).

Apart from other differences or considerations, ch. 1 differs from chs. 2, 3 and 4 in that it follows the order of the alphabet which has come down to us, with *ayin* (v. 16) before *pe* (v. 17), whereas chs. 2, 3 and 4 have the verses beginning with *pe* before those beginning with *ayin*. In this connection we should note that the person who placed the *aleph, bet* and so on above the units in the Septuagint (and the Vulgate) is unlikely to have been the translator, for the *ayin* has been placed above the *pe* verse and vice versa in these three chapters, though this has been corrected in some manuscripts. That this may reflect a different alphabetic order is seen from an examination of Ps. 34.16 (ET 15) (*ayin*), 17 (ET 16) (*pe*), where scholars feel that the sense dictates that the original order of the verses was 17, 16 (ET 16, 15). It has been suggested that this demonstrates that the author of ch. 1 of Lamentations is different from the author of chs. 2, 3 and 4. While this may be so, the differences in the texts may be due to different processes of transmission, for if scholars are right about Psalm 34, the present text has been adjusted to suit an order acceptable to collector or editor. In the case of Lamentations, transposition of the verses does not affect progression of thought.

This alphabetic acrostic style is by no means unique to the Old Testament. The device was employed in Mesopotamia and Egypt and also in the Hellenistic and Roman periods (see Marcus and Pfeiffer). But why did our poet (or poets) employ this device in these poems? Why not give reign to spontaneity? Why go to the bother of confining one's passionate thoughts in the straitjacket of the acrostic form?

One suggestion is that the purpose of the form was to teach the alphabet. (Luther called Ps. 119 'the golden ABCE'.) The jingle 'A is for apple so rosy and red; B is for boy and also for bed...' is one way of instilling in the modern child the names and order (and function?) of the letters of the alphabet. Are we witnessing an ancient example of the same thing in these poems? This suggestion has few adherents. To begin with, this is not literature for children or for unschooled and ignorant adults. It is quite sophisticated poetry. Secondly, the alphabet is only discernible visually. Listening to the poems (with the possible exception of ch. 3) one would be hard pressed to recognize the device; it is only when one looks at the text that one is aware of it. In the case of ch. 3 it is more obvious in that

4. The Poetry of Lamentations

every three lines begins with the same letter; but in chs. 1, 2 and 4 it does not impose itself (for instance in ch. 1 only one line in three begins with the relevant letter). It might be argued that the *origin* of the form was indeed to teach the alphabet to children, but one must conclude that this was not the purpose of these poems (cf. Munch).

Some have argued that the purpose of the acrostic was to endeavour to control magical power. It is common knowledge that certain language forms—particular phrases and words, spells and exorcisms—have been widely used in various cultures to ensure that evil was kept at bay and that blessings were received. It was pointed out by Jeremias that in ancient Babylonia the entire alphabet represented the cosmic circle and so was thought to possess supernatural power, and that in ancient Israel there may have been a belief that the letters of the alphabet had a special divine power. To employ them in sequence would, therefore, lend power to one's composition, but as Gottwald observes, there is no evidence whatever that the Israelites of this period held such beliefs, although they are to be found on the outskirts of mediaeval Judaism. However, the fact that we have Hebrew letters placed above text units in the Septuagint makes one wonder if it was felt, at a very early stage, that they were thought to have some mystical significance. The fact that Tallis, in setting Lam. 1.1-5 to music in the sixteenth century, devoted no fewer than sixteen bars to the singing of the word *aleph* may point in the same direction! But these responses or interpretations may totally misrepresent the original intention.

Another theory is that the device was employed as an aid to memory. One might be better able to memorize a passage, poem or list if one had the help of a sequence of letters. On the surface this is a plausible theory, but this may be because we ourselves have used the sequence as a memory aid. It is just possible that the alphabetic acrostic form did originally have this aim, but can it be argued that this is what is at work in Lamentations? If the 22 letters of the Hebrew alphabet had appeared in sequence only once in the book and if it is assumed that the book is a literary unit, then one might conclude that the 22 letters were the initial sounds indicating to the mourners the beginning of the 22 sections of the book. But such is not the case. We have the 22 letters used in sequence four times in the book, so people reciting the text are not helped much if they cannot remember which of the *bets*, say, they are presently at! The situation is not helped by the progressions of thought in each poem.

Of course, as Gottwald notes, if the book is not a literary unit and the poems were composed separately, the mnemonic theory seems more credible. The poems might have been composed in the acrostic manner to aid memory. It was only when they were brought together that the alphabetic confusion would have arisen.

Related loosely to the second suggestion, above, is the theory, originating with De Wette, that the purpose of the acrostic was to convey completeness in the author's expression of grief. This view has been picked up and expressed differently by a number of scholars. The last word, the ultimate in confession or in lament, can only be achieved if all the letters in the alphabet are used; and the tidiness of the acrostic serves to emphasize this. Gottwald refers to the Babylonian Talmud (*b. Šab.* 55a), where there is a reference to 'the people who fulfil the Torah from *aleph* to *taw*', and he uses this to buttress his argument. The author of the Lamentations acrostic

> wanted to bring about a complete cleansing of the conscience through a total confession of sin. Even then his purpose was not spent. He was also determined to inculcate an attitude of submission and a prospect of hope. By intimately binding together the themes of sin, suffering, submission and hope, he intended to implant the conviction of trust and confidence in the goodness and imminent intervention of Yahweh. That this is the case is evident in the third poem where the acrostic form is intensified at precisely the point where hope becomes the strongest.

There may be something in what Gottwald says, but there is a weakness in his position. If the author had 'complete confession' in mind, why did he not list the sins committed? Although the poet confesses the guilt of Israel and acknowledges that Yahweh has punished the people accordingly, he does not itemize the sins. He speaks only in general terms: 1.8, 'Jerusalem sinned grievously'; 1.18, 'I have rebelled against

4. The Poetry of Lamentations

his word', 1.20, 'I have been very rebellious'; 1.22, 'All my transgressions'; 3.42, 'We have transgressed and rebelled'; 4.6, 'the iniquity of the daughter of my people is greater than the sin of Sodom'; 4.13, 'The sins of her prophets, the iniquities of her priests who shed in the midst of her the blood of the righteous'; 5.7, 'Our fathers sinned'; 5.16, 'We have sinned'. If what Gottwald claims is correct we should have expected lists of transgressions and iniquities and sins; but we do not find this. We might have expected specific acts of rebellion to be mentioned; but apart from the allusion to prophets and priests shedding the blood of the righteous (4.13), the very few references to sins are in such general terms that it might be deduced that the poet was not conscious of *specific* wrongdoing.

The final possibility is that the acrostic is simply an artistic device (like the sonnet, for example) and one which was imitated by the authors of Psalms 9, 10, 34 and 119, all of which are probably later than Lamentations (cf. Anderson, who thinks that the author of the Lamentations acrostic had few, if any, Hebrew prototypes at hand). Hillers points out that the book of Lamentations puts into poetry what 2 Kings expresses in prose; and it may be that, being skilled in composing poetry, our poet was anxious to show his ability further by using the *qînâ* metre, and still more by this alphabetic acrostic form. The *aleph* to *taw* reference in the Talmud may simply be an early interpretation of the acrostic, with which suggestion Gottwald agrees.

Further Reading

K. Budde, 'Poetry', *HDB*, IV, pp. 2-13.

W.M.L. De Wette, *A Critical and Historical Introduction to the Canonical Scriptures of the Old Testament*, II (Boston: Little, Brown, 1858), pp. 530-32.

Eissfeldt, *The Old Testament: An Introduction*, pp. 500-505.

D.N. Freedman, 'Acrostics and Metrics in Hebrew Poetry', *HTR* 65 (1972), pp. 367-92.

—'Acrostic Poems in the Hebrew Bible: Alphabetic and Otherwise', *CBQ* 48 (1986), pp. 408-31.

W.R. Garr, 'The Qinah: A Study of Poetic Meter, Syntax and Style', *ZAW* 95 (1983), pp. 54-75.

Gottwald, *Studies in the Book of Lamentations*, pp. 23-32.

G.B. Gray, *The Forms of Hebrew Poetry* (London: Hodder & Stoughton, 1915).
Hillers, *Lamentations*, pp. 18-31.
A. Jeremias, *Das Alte Testament im Lichte des Alten Orients* (Leipzig: Hinrichs, 4th edn, 1930).
R.A. Knox, *The Holy Bible* (London: Burns & Oates, 1955).
M. Löhr, 'Alphabetische und alphabetisierende Lieder im Alten Testament', *ZAW* 25 (1905), pp. 173-98.
R. Marcus, 'Alphabetic Acrostics in the Hellenistic and Roman Periods', *JNES* 6 (1947), pp. 109-15.
P.A. Munch, 'Die alphabetische Akrostischie in der jüdischen Psalmendichtung', *ZDMG* 90 (1936), pp. 703-10.
R.H. Pfeiffer, 'A Dialogue with Human Misery', *ANET*, pp. 438ff.
W.H. Shea, 'The *qinah* Structure of the Book of Lamentations', *Bib* 60 (1979), pp. 103-107.
W.G.E. Watson, *Classical Hebrew Poetry: A Guide to its Techniques* (JSOTSup, 26; Sheffield: JSOT Press, 1984).

5
AUTHORSHIP

The Connection with Jeremiah

AS MENTIONED IN THE INTRODUCTION, the view that Jeremiah was the author of Lamentations is not now held by the majority of scholars. It is clear from the title given to the book in various translations and commentaries that whereas the name of Jeremiah *was* closely associated with Lamentations in the distant and not too distant past, the tendency nowadays is to question that association.

The Coverdale Bible (1535) and the Authorized Version (1611) both entitle the book 'The Lamentations of Jeremiah'. Furthermore, commentators were inclined to take Jeremian authorship for granted. B. Blayney's 1784 commentary on the book (bound together with that on Jeremiah) has the title *The Lamentations of Jeremiah* and in the introduction the author does not even raise the question of authorship. This consensus was beginning to change by the time of A.W. Streane's commentary of 1881; although Streane agrees with Blayney he does at least raise the question of authorship. He ends his discussion with the words, 'On the whole therefore we conclude that Jeremiah was beyond question the writer of the Book'.

It would seem, therefore, that the first questioning of the authorship of the book by H. von der Hardt in 1712 (cited by Ricciotti) had fallen on deaf ears, and that the old tradition had continued to be the accepted norm. Translations appearing as late as 1952 (RSV) continued to imply Jeremian authorship. However, more recent translations (NEB, JB, REB, NRSV, NIV) and commentators (Meek, Hillers, Kraus) no longer follow this style. If modern scholarship is correct in severing

Lamentations' connections with Jeremiah, how did that link come about in the first place and in what circumstances?

There is no doubt that the tradition is ancient. The Septuagint version of Lamentations begins: 'When Israel was taken captive, and Jerusalem made desolate, Jeremiah sat weeping, and lamented with this lamentation over Jerusalem, and said...'; and scholars agree that the Greek style here demonstrates that this is an actual translation from Hebrew; in other words, it was not simply added in the Greek transmission of the text. If, as seems likely, the translation into Greek took place before the end of the second century BCE, it follows that already at that time there was a strong tradition that Jeremiah was the author of Lamentations.

The Septuagint's grouping of the books of the Old Testament differs at times from that of the Hebrew (for instance Ruth appears in the Megillot in the Hebrew text but after Judges in the Greek version), and in the case of Lamentations this is quite significant. Whereas in the Hebrew text the book is in the Megillot, in the Septuagint it stands immediately after the book of Jeremiah, a further indication of the strength of the tradition of authorship.

This tradition is indeed a strong and persistent one. So the Vulgate (Latin version) begins:

> After Israel was led into captivity and Jerusalem laid waste, Jeremiah the prophet sat weeping, and lamented with this lamentation over Jerusalem. And with a sorrowful mind, sighing and moaning, he said...

The Peshitta (Syriac version) entitles the book 'The Lamentations of Jeremiah', while the Targum (Aramaic paraphrase) begins: 'Jeremiah the Prophet and High Priest said...' The Church Fathers follow the tradition attested by the book's position after Jeremiah in the Septuagint and Vulgate. We may also compare the Babylonian Talmud: 'Jeremiah wrote the book of his name, Kings and Lamentations' (*b. B. Bat.* 15a). Luther entitled the book 'Die Klagelieder der Jeremias' and Calvin did not raise the question of authorship. So in the history of the book's interpretation there has been a substantial body of opinion which has held to Jeremian authorship;

5. Authorship

the view that Jeremiah was not the author is comparatively recent. It should be noted that the Hebrew text of Lamentations makes no mention of Jeremiah, and in the Hebrew Bible the book stands in the Megillot and not after Jeremiah. Since it is difficult to imagine Jeremiah's name having been left out in transmission—the name is more likely to have been added—it is possible that the Hebrew text preserves the more original tradition. Furthermore, the fact that in the Hebrew Bible the book is not juxtaposed with Jeremiah may be a further indication that at an earlier stage it was not associated with the prophet.

How, then, did the book come to be linked with Jeremiah? It is very likely that the origin of this tradition lies in 2 Chron. 35.25:

> And Jeremiah lamented for Josiah; and all the singing men and singing women spoke of Josiah in their laments, unto this day; and they made them an ordinance in Israel; and, behold, they are written in the Laments.

Indeed, the Catholic Biblical Association of America translation actually renders the last word 'Lamentations', thereby linking this passage with the book in the Hebrew Bible. Furthermore, Lam. 4.20, although probably alluding to the king Zedekiah, was interpreted by the early commentators as referring to Josiah; and this would have consolidated the link with Jeremiah.

If this was the origin of the tradition, it probably arose in the time when it was thought important to have names of ancient worthies attached to literature. In the Pseudepigraphic literature the names of, for example, Adam and Eve or Solomon were associated with works with a view to enhancing their value. Moses, the lawgiver, becomes the source of Israelite law, David the author of all Psalms (cf. Russell).

The association with Jeremiah may have been strengthened by the tone of passages like Jer. 8.18-22; 9; 14; 15) which are, to some degree, reminiscent of Lamentations. Furthermore, some have argued that passages such as Lam. 3.14, 53-56 fit neatly with or, indeed, refer back to incidents in Jeremiah's life (cf. Jer. 20.7; 38.6-8). Driver felt that these 'similarities' may have been the origin of the tradition. It may have been thought that Lamentations must have been written by someone who had experienced the fall of Jerusalem and, at least, the subsequent hardships, and that the prophet Jeremiah, who had been present at that time and who had agonized over the imminent collapse of Judah, was the most probable author.

One of the strongest arguments in favour of Jeremian authorship is that the disaster is presented in both books as the result of national sin (compare Lam. 1.5 with Jer. 26). This is an important argument, but it is not conclusive. We may suppose from this comparison that the author of Lamentations was following in the footsteps of, or was in agreement with, Jeremiah, but we may perhaps go no further than that. Again, there is the observation that the sympathetic outpouring of emotion on behalf of the nation, which is clear in Lamentations, is also found in Jeremiah (for example in Jer. 14–15). Thirdly, some scholars have drawn attention to similarities of expression in both books. Thus the phrase 'eyes flow down with tears' (1.16; 2.11; 3.48-49) is echoed in Jeremiah (9.1, 18; 13.17; 14.17); the phrase 'terror on every side' (2.22) is found in Jeremiah (6.25); and the reference to the 'sins of the prophets and priests' (2.14; 4.13) is shared with Jeremiah (2.8; 5.31; 14.13-14; 23.11).

On the other hand, some scholars are convinced that the evidence points in the opposite direction; that Jeremiah could not have written Lamentations. It is pointed out that Lamentations has a vocabulary which differs from that of Jeremiah. One might however respond to this by drawing attention to the fact that Jeremiah is prophecy while Lamentations is psalmody; if a writer of prose fiction turns to write poetry about his or her personal life, the vocabulary used will inevitably be different. So the argument from vocabulary is inconclusive. Perhaps more convincing is the evidence from the contents of the book. If, for example, we look at Jer. 2.18, where Jeremiah appears to be scathing about Egypt, or, again, at 2.36, where he expects Egypt to be hostile to Israel (cf. also 37.5-10), and compare this passage with Lam. 4.17, 'Our eyes failed, ever watching vainly for

5. Authorship

help; in our watching we watched for a nation which could not save' (which most scholars take to be a reference to Egypt) we must surely conclude that the latter passage could hardly have been written by Jeremiah. Again, if Lam. 4.19-20 refers to the flight (prior to the fall of Jerusalem) of Zedekiah and his entourage, described in 2 Kgs 25.4-5, it would seem that the author was in the royal party, whereas Jer. 38.28 implies that Jeremiah was in custody at that time.

It would seem, therefore, that it is difficult to sustain the tradition that Jeremiah wrote Lamentations. (In ancient times the question of authorship was not investigated as it is today. For many, it was not important, and we know very little about the authorship of any of the books in the Hebrew Bible). But if not Jeremiah, who did write the book? Was there, in fact, only one author, or was there more than one?

Some of the arguments adduced against Jeremian authorship lead one to consider the possibility that Lamentations was not written by a single author. For example, the fact that the order of the alphabet in ch. 1 is different from that in chs. 2, 3 and 4 suggests that the author of ch. 1 may have been different from the author of chs. 2, 3 and 4. The fact that ch. 5 is the only poem which is not an acrostic, has a different metre from chs. 1–4 and is in the form of a prayer, while the others are not, are points worthy of note (cf. Lachs). Chapter 3 differs in genre from chs. 1, 2, 4 and 5 (see below) and this too has a bearing on the debate. Again, if the argument that ch. 1 was written just after 597 BCE, and not after the fall of Jerusalem in 586 BCE, is sustained, the case for single authorship is further weakened. Finally, we might ask why we should think in terms of a single author for a collection of poems which makes no claims as regards authorship. If the book of Psalms, once thought to be the work of David, can be thought of as a collection of poems by various writers, why not the collection we call Lamentations?

On the other hand, there are factors which might tell in favour of single authorship. The fact that, unlike the book of Psalms, all five poems appear to be dealing with the same period is important. Most scholars tend to interpret the sharpness and vividness of expression in Lamentations as evidence that the author was contemporary with the events he describes, and this is significant. If, as 2 Kgs 25.12 indicates, those left behind in Judah were the poorest of the land, the number of eye-witnesses sophisticated enough to write these poems must have been very small indeed; poets of this calibre will have been thin on the ground. It is also worth noting here that there are no marked differences between the poems in terms of their ideas and theology.

Provenance

The first thing that comes to mind in this connection is the continuity with the pre-exilic prophetic voice. Time and again throughout the poems the sentiments echo those of Isaiah, Jeremiah, Micah and the like. The doom envisaged by the prophets in relation to the sin of the people of Yahweh is picked up in the various poems and handled in a way which makes one wonder whether the author is from the prophetic element in society. He reflects on the connection between the catastrophe he describes and on people's responsibility for it. Again, in interpreting the disaster as the work of Yahweh, who is in control, he stands in the prophetic line; similarly, the hope that shines out of the negative experiences appears to reflect a faith which we find in the prophetic literature. On the other hand, the concern that the author shows for the Temple, the altar and the festivals might point in the direction of the priestly circles. Some, on the strength of 4.19-20, have supposed that the author was neither prophet nor priest (cf. 4.13) but a layman and a member of the royal court.

Date

As I have already indicated, I concur with the view that Lamentations was written shortly after 586 BCE, in the aftermath of the collapse of the state of Judah and the city of Jerusalem. The horrific scenes to which the author alludes and describes again and again indicate that he is an eye-witness who is still experiencing the horrors and the devastation. Hillers rightly points out that the kind of hope that

5. Authorship

appeared in later exilic times had not yet raised its head. The fact that ch. 1 does not refer to the actual destruction of the city led Rudolph to the conclusion that it was written after the events of 597 BCE. This remains a possibility, although one might argue that the devastation referred to in ch. 1 is too severe to reflect only the setback of 597 BCE.

Place of Composition

While it is impossible to be certain of the location of our author, it should be noted that each poem reflects the tragic situation in Judah. The abundant references to Jerusalem or Zion and the absence of specific references to Babylon would seem to point in the same direction. Indeed, the statement at 1.3 that Judah 'dwells now among the nations, but finds no resting place' should probably be understood to have been written from the standpoint of Judah.

Further Reading

B. Blayney, *Jeremiah and Lamentations* (Oxford: Oxford University Press, 1784).
G. Brunet, *Les Lamentations contre Jérémie: Réinterpretation des quatre premières lamentations* (Bibliothèque de l'Ecole des Hautes Etudes, Section des Sciences Religieuses, 75; Paris: Presses Universitaires de France, 1968).
W.W. Cannon, 'The Authorship of Lamentations', *BS* 81 (1924), pp. 42-58.
S.R. Driver, *Introduction to the Literature of the Old Testament* (Edinburgh: T. & T. Clark, 7th edn, 1898), pp. 456-65.
S.A. Fries, 'Parallele zwischen den Klageliedern Cap. IV, V und der Maccabäerzeit', *ZAW* 13 (1893), pp. 110-24.
S.T. Lachs, 'The Date of Lamentations V', *JQR* NS 57 (1966–67), pp. 46-56.
M. Löhr, 'Threni III und die jeremianische Autorsschaft des Buchs der Klagelieder', *ZAW* 24 (1904), pp. 1-16.
Meek, 'The Book of Lamentations', pp. 1-38.
Nägelsbach, *The Lamentations of Jeremiah*, esp. pp. 6-16; cf. pp. 19-35!
G. Ricciotti, *Le Lamentazioni de Geremia* (Rome, 1924).

D.S. Russell, *From Early Judaism to Early Church* (Philadelphia: Fortress Press, 1986).

Streane, *Jeremiah, Lamentations*, pp. 353-58.

H. Wiesmann, 'Der Verfasser des Büchleins der Klagelieder ein Augenzeuge der behandelten Ereignisse?', *Bib* 17 (1936), pp. 71-84.

See also the introductions to the various commentaries.

6
GENRE

IT IS CLEAR EVEN on a first reading that the book of Lamentations is reminiscent of the book of Psalms. Earlier this century H. Gunkel analysed the psalms according to their respective types (*Gattungen*), and this work was continued by W. Baumgartner, H. Jahnow and others. It was discovered that there are five main categories: hymns, communal laments, royal psalms, individual laments and individual thanksgiving psalms, in addition to less common types such as entrance liturgies and pilgrimage psalms, and others which appear to display various forms (what Gunkel called mixed poems). These scholars agreed that these types are not confined, in the Old Testament, to the book of Psalms but are to be found elsewhere, for instance in the book of Lamentations.

The type of psalm which most readily comes to mind for Lamentations is the communal lament, in that the initial impression conveyed by the book is of a grief-stricken community; indeed, the fifth poem conforms quite closely to those psalms in the Psalter which are usually placed in this category, such as Psalms 74, 79 and 89. Communal laments appear to have been composed and recited on occasions of national disaster, military or natural, and also to commemorate such events. It is usual, in these laments, for the people to complain to God about their plight and to plead with him for relief or deliverance. Although ch. 5 is closest in shape to the other psalms of communal lament in the book of Psalms, it is correct to say, as does Gottwald, that all five poems have that flavour. The other four chapters of Lamentations fall into Gunkel's category of 'mixed poems', since they exhibit or draw on elements from at least three recognizable types: the individual lament, the communal lament and the funeral song or dirge.

The funeral song or dirge is, in its simplest form, the utterance of the bereaved at the bier or at the burial of the deceased. It probably varied considerably from one community to another in the ancient Near East, only later taking on fixed forms; but it has, as essential elements, the cry of despair (in Hebrew, *'êkâ*, 'ah!' and 'how!'), the statement of death, the name of the deceased, the contrast between 'then' and 'now', and the call to weep. In the Old Testament the funeral dirge is rare. References are made to it, as when Abraham mourns the death of Sarah (Gen. 23.2); occasionally we get a fragment of such a dirge, as when David mourns the death of Abner (2 Sam. 3.33-34). The fullest example is the passage in 2 Sam. 1.17-27 where David mourns for Saul and Jonathan: 'How are the mighty fallen...! Beloved and lovely were Saul and Jonathan...Daughters of Israel, weep for Saul... I grieve for you, my brother Jonathan; you were most dear to me'.

In the course of time the dirge came to be applied to the demise of communities—cities and tribes—their downfall being interpreted as death. In the Old Testament this device is seen in Amos: 'Fallen, no more to rise, is the virgin Israel; forsaken on her land, with none to raise her up' (Amos 5.2; cf. Jer. 9.20-21), although in the hands of the prophet the form is used *before* the fall in order to shock the audience. The funeral song focuses on death and misery. By contrast, the lament proper, although it may have death as its occasion, concentrates on life, and is often in the form of a prayer to God, confessing sins, expressing trust and pleading for help (for example Ps. 79).

Eissfeldt classifies chs. 1, 2, and 4 of Lamentations as funeral dirges with political application. It is true that these three poems begin with the characteristic cry 'How' (cf. 2 Sam. 1.25, 27) and initially proceed as in a dirge; but, taken as a whole, these poems are not merely political funeral dirges: they are a mixture of forms. Thus in ch. 1 we find that vv. 1-11, 17 are a dirge over the fall of Jerusalem, but in vv. 9c, 11c we have snippets which fall outside the character of the dirge,

6. Genre

in that Jerusalem *herself* speaks and describes her pain and sorrow. These fragments, together with vv. 12-22, are in the form of an individual lament. But while the forms are different, interpretation is not a problem: both forms serve the same purpose. It is true that Jerusalem is not dead, but the author may have chosen the dirge as a vehicle of communication because the tragedy, which he has experienced and which Jerusalem has experienced, is best conveyed in extreme terms; besides, death was all around him. As Gottwald says, 'Before his very eyes the mourning rites are observed for the dead inhabitants of the city' (2.10). This suggests to him the figure of the city 'as a widow', which refers quite as much to her social dispossession as to her loss of nearest kin: 'We are not to look for a literal "husband"'.

By describing the plight of Jerusalem in extravagant language and in the form of a funeral song, and combining this with lamentation placed in the mouth of Jerusalem herself, the author ensures the maximum effect for his poem. The overall intention is communal and national.

The second poem is similar to the first: it is a mixture of forms. The original character of the dirge as a secular wail is apparent in 1.1-11, where there is only an occasional allusion to God's involvement in the catastrophe. In ch. 2 the dirge form has been further transformed in that God is brought in much earlier and more comprehensively. Indeed, it is not just disaster which is lamented: it is *God's* disaster, as vv. 1-9 and 17 make clear. However, the sudden appearance of the poet's voice in vv. 13-17, addressing Jerusalem, is in keeping with the funeral song style as attested in 2 Sam. 1.26, where David addresses the dead Jonathan directly. Indeed, Lam. 2.13, 'What can I say for you, to what compare you, O daughter of Jerusalem? What can I liken to you, that I may comfort you, O virgin daughter of Zion? For vast as the sea is your ruin; who can restore you?', is reminiscent of that verse: 'I am distressed for you, my brother Jonathan; very pleasant have you been to me; your love to me was wonderful, passing the love of women'. When the poet calls on Jerusalem to pray, the funeral song experiences yet another transformation; the poet himself complains to Yahweh about the extreme nature of the disaster and then, as in ch. 1, the personified Jerusalem responds in the form of an individual lament.

In ch. 4 the poet again employs the funeral dirge as his basic form. After the initial cry, the poem continues as in ch. 1 with descriptions of various scenes of distress and desperation, alluding to the past as compared to the present. The author next introduces the communal lament in the first person plural (vv. 17-20), and then, in prophetic style, addresses Edom (v. 21) and Zion (v. 22) in a quite different mood. It is sometimes argued that the explanation of the transition from gloom to assurance in psalms of lament is to be found in an oracle by a priest (or cultic prophet), who responds to the afflicted petitioner (for example, Ps. 6.7 reads: 'My eye wastes away because of grief...', while v. 8 reads: 'Depart from me, all you workers of evil; for the Lord has heard the sound of my weeping'). Perhaps the final verses in ch. 4 are modelled on such an oracle.

Chapter 3 is the most difficult of the poems to interpret, and the question of its genre is likewise not straightforward. Unlike chs. 1, 2, and 4 this chapter has no links with the funeral dirge; but is it an individual lament or a communal lament? At first glance it looks very like an individual lament in that it begins in the first person singular and, indeed, continues in that mode for the first 39 verses. We then have a passage in the first person plural (vv. 40-47) which appears to be in the form of a communal lament. Finally there is a return to the first person singular in vv. 48-66 which, again, might be taken as being in the form of the individual lament.

In the early history of interpretation questions of this kind were generally not asked. If Jeremiah was the author, then 'I am the man' (v. 1) referred to Jeremiah: this poem was an individual lament which, because of Jeremiah's feeling for his people, burst forth into a communal lament. Since the questioning of Jeremian authorship, the identification of the 'man' in ch. 3 has occasioned great interest and speculation. Some continue to understand the 'man' as Jeremiah (Löhr, Rudolph, Meek) although they do not hold that Jeremiah wrote the poem, believing rather that the authorial intention was to *present* Jeremiah as the writer. Others go further and

6. Genre

see the chapter as a poem about the troubles of an *unknown* sufferer, an individual lament which has nothing to do with the other poems and is not concerned with the fall of Jerusalem in 586 BCE (Stade). Still others have tried to identify the 'man' with a historical figure such as King Jehoiachin (Porteous).

Another variation on the individual interpretation is that of Hillers, who takes the view that the 'man' is not a specific historical figure but rather anyone who has greatly suffered:

> He is an 'Everyman', a figure who represents what any man may feel when it seems that God is against him. Through this representative sufferer the poet points the way to the nation, as he shows the man who has been through trouble moving into, then out of, near despair to patient faith and penitence, thus becoming a model for the nation.

There may be something in what Hillers says here, but one of the difficulties with the individual interpretation, whatever form it takes, is the transition from first person singular to first person plural in vv. 40-47.

The final individual interpretation is that the 'I' is the poet himself. As Davidson suggests, 'He is responding to the hurt and bitter cry of Zion at the end of the last chapter, by reliving his own experience which took him to the verge of despair before he came to terms with it'.

Perhaps a more natural way of understanding the poem is a collective interpretation. Eissfeldt argues:

> In spite of the fact that the poem is in large measure in the form of the individual song of lamentation, there ought never to have been any doubt that it was composed from the first with reference to the disaster to Jerusalem. Even the fact that it begins *I am the man*, whereas elsewhere Jerusalem is normally referred to in the feminine as the city, does not provide an argument against this. For on the one hand the change over to 'We' (vv. 40-47) can only be understood if the poet had from the outset a plural entity in mind, Jerusalem or Judah, and on the other hand, the placing of the third poem with the others which clearly apply to the disaster to Jerusalem, represents at the very least the oldest commentary upon the poem that we have. There is no reason for trusting the oldest commentary less than later explanations and modern feelings.

The debate continues, although Eissfeldt's arguments are, perhaps, the most attractive. It is probable that we have here an individual lament but with a communal intention, and if this is the case it is in line with the other four poems.

Possible Mesopotamian Influence

The discovery of laments from ancient Mesopotamia has led to some speculation as to the influence these may have had on the Old Testament and, in particular, on the book of Lamentations. Do these poems (or at least chs. 1, 2 and 4) derive from a genre current in Mesopotamia?

In the 1950s and later there was great interest in establishing the connection between the literature of Mesopotamia and the Old Testament. Kramer writes:

> There is little doubt that it was the Sumerian poets who originated and developed the 'lamentation' genre—there are Sumerian examples dating possibly from as early as the Third Dynasty of Ur... and that the Biblical Book of Lamentations, as well as the 'burden' laments of the prophets, represent a profoundly moving transformation of the more formal and conventional Mesopotamian prototypes.

Gadd is also quite convinced that Lamentations is 'manifestly under the influence' of Sumerian laments.

Not all scholars are as positive as this. Ancient Mesopotamian literature may have found its way westwards, but it is difficult to establish any direct link between its laments and our book of Lamentations (cf. Tigay). The fact that we have laments in both cultures does not argue for direct borrowing or even influence, for as Rudolph says, such similarities may be merely due to similar experiences. In 1968 McDaniel examined alleged parallels between Lamentations and the lament over the destruction of Ur and concluded that they were not definite enough to be evidence of a relationship between the two texts. It has been alleged, for example, that the language of Lam. 1.3b, 5 is similar to that of lUr 306-308: 'I am one who has been exiled from the city, I am one who has found no rest... I am one who has been exiled from his house, I am one who has found no dwelling place'. At first a

6. Genre

direct connection seems plausible, but on closer examination we note that whereas in Lamentations the reference is to Judah's exile, in the Ur lamentation the reference is to a goddess! It makes better sense to see in Lamentations a reference to Deut. 28.64-65: 'The Lord will scatter you among all peoples...among these nations you shall find no ease, and there shall be no rest for the sole of your foot'. McDaniel's article provides further examples. Subsequent to McDaniel's work, Gwaltney has argued that such parallels do exist, that they are strong, and that the connecting link was the exile, the period when Israel encountered the Mesopotamian city-laments.

Hillers, who was undecided in the first edition (1972) of his commentary, comes out more strongly in his 1992 edition, where he devotes a section of his introduction to 'Lamentations and the City-Lament Tradition'. Although not dogmatic, he now argues that the resemblances between the Mesopotamian laments and Lamentations are evidence of 'some kind of connection'; and he suggests that there may have been a city-lament tradition within Israel as far back as the earliest prophetic writings, although he admits that he is trying to reconstruct 'a dinosaur out of bits of fossil'. If Hillers is right, the view of many commentators that Lamentations 1, 2 and 4 represent funeral dirges is, perhaps, called into question; but Hillers has an uphill task to argue his case here.

Further Reading

Albrektson, *Studies in the Text and Theology of the Book of Lamentations*, pp. 126ff.
Eissfeldt, *The Old Testament: An Introduction*, pp. 94-98, 501-503.
C.J. Gadd, 'The Second Lamentation for Ur', in D.W. Thomas and W.D. McHardy (eds.), *Hebrew and Semitic Studies* (Oxford: Oxford University Press, pp. 59-71.
T.H. Gaster, *Myth, Legend and Custom in the Old Testament* (New York: Harper & Row, 1969), pp. 815-28.
Gottwald, *Studies in the Book of Lamentations*, pp. 33-46.
H. Gunkel and J. Begrich, *Einleitung in die Psalmen* (Göttingen: Vandenhoeck & Ruprecht, 1933).
W.C. Gwaltney, 'The Biblical Book of Lamentations in the Context of

Near Eastern Lament Literature', in W. Hallo, J. Moyer and L. Perdue (eds.), *Scripture in Context II: More Essays on the Comparative Method* (Winona Lake, IN: Eisenbrauns, 1983), pp. 191-211.

Hillers, *Lamentations*, pp. 32-39.

H. Jahnow, *Das hebräische Leichenlied im Rahmen der Völkerdichtung* (BZAW, 36, 1923).

S.N. Kramer, 'Lamentation over the Destruction of Ur', *ANET*, pp. 455-63.

—'Sumerian Literature and the Bible', in *Studia Biblica et Orientalia*. III. *Oriens Antiquus* (AnBib, 12; Rome: Biblical Institute Press, 1959).

Kraus, *Klagelieder*.

T.F. McDaniel, 'The Alleged Sumerian Influence upon Lamentations', *VT* 18 (1968), pp. 198-209.

N.W. Porteous, 'Jerusalem-Zion: The Growth of a Symbol', in A. Kuschke (ed.), *Verbannung und Heimkehr* (Tübingen: Mohr, 1961), pp. 235-52.

C. Westermann, *Praise and Lament in the Psalms* (Edinburgh: T. & T. Clark: Atlanta: John Knox, 1981).

—'Lamentations', in B.W. Anderson (ed.), *Books of the Bible*. I. *The Old Testament / The Hebrew Bible* (New York: Macmillan, 1989), pp. 303-18.

7
THE THEOLOGY OF THE BOOK

IT IS DEBATABLE WHETHER the book of Lamentations has an overall distinctive theology, though there is no doubt that theological ideas are to be found there in abundance. For example, even a cursory reading will reveal that views are expressed about God's justice and mercy; and the disaster in the background is interpreted in terms of God's action and the sin of the people.

Gottwald argued that the book is, like Job, about suffering, although unlike Job, which is not given a historical setting, Lamentations is closely connected with historical crisis. What exercises the poet is the problem of the old doctrine of reward and punishment, clearly expressed in Deuteronomy. This stated that if Israel obeyed God's law they would have peace and prosperity; if, on the other hand, they disobeyed, they would experience adversity. The problem for the poet was posed by a series of disasters from the death of the good king Josiah in 609 BCE to the catastrophe of 586 BCE. Why did Josiah's righteous ways end in what turned out to be the most disastrous period in the history of the people of Yahweh? Gottwald argues that we find 'the situational key to the theology of Lamentations in the tension between Deuteronomic faith and historical adversity'.

There is no doubt that the fall of Jerusalem was the most momentous event in the history of Israel, and the implications for Yahwism and for the history and religious life of the people were wide and far-reaching. The questioning on the lines that Gottwald imagines must have surfaced during

Manasseh's reign. In Manasseh's case the problem was: why should such an evil king reign or live for such a long time? And the question would become more acute with Josiah's death (cf. Salters). Indeed, the questioning would have reached its height at that point. After Josiah the clean edges of the argument would have become somewhat blurred with the reigns of Jehoiakim, Jehoiachin and Zedekiah. By 586 BCE, although, no doubt, the queries still had some way to run, they would not be asked with such conviction. As Albrektson pointed out,

> only if you think that the people have really trodden the paths of righteousness can you see a contradiction between the retribution pattern and the fact that the people have been stricken by the catastrophe. But this view of the people's relationship with God cannot be established in the book of Lamentations.

Indeed, there are several references there to the view of the calamity as a punishment by Yahweh for the sins of the people (for example 1.5, 8, 18).

Albrektson claimed that there is a tension in the book involving the Jerusalem tradition of the inviolability of Zion and the historical reality of the destruction of the city. This tradition is clearly seen in Ps. 46.5: 'God is in the midst of her, she shall not be moved; God will help her right early'. But it is also found in Psalms 48 and 76, and it is this tradition which Jeremiah also encountered and attacked (see Jer. 7 and 26).

As most commentators agree that the author of Lamentations was from Jerusalem, we may assume that he would have been very aware of this doctrine, and Albrektson tries to show that he often alludes to it in various phrases. Perhaps the clearest such reference is at 4.12, where we read: 'the kings of the earth did not believe, or any of the inhabitants of the world, that foe or enemy could enter the gates of Jerusalem'.

Albrektson then compares the text of Lamentations with that of Deuteronomy 28 and concludes that the poet had that chapter in mind. The examples chosen are interesting and, if it could be demonstrated that Deuteronomy 28 predates Lamentations, almost convincing. The example used by

7. The Theology of the Book   111

Albrektson is Lam. 1.3: 'She dwells among the nations, but find no resting place'. This recalls a passage in Deut. 28.64-65:

> And the Lord will scatter you among the peoples, from one end of the earth to the other; and there you shall serve other gods of wood and stone which neither you nor your fathers have known. And among these nations you shall find no ease, and there shall be no rest for the sole of your foot...

But there are many other possible allusions to Deuteronomy 28 in Lamentations, and Albrektson feels these cannot be coincidental. What has happened, he argues, is that the author of Lamentations used Deuteronomy 28 in his description of the situation after 586 BCE in such a way as to give a theological interpretation of the catastrophe. What had happened must be understood as God's punishment for the sins of the people. Finally, he cites Lam. 2.17: 'The Lord has done what he purposed, he has carried out his threat; as he ordained long ago, he has demolished without pity', arguing that here we have a passage which harks back to earlier traditions which had predicted the calamity. Hence, for Albrektson, the Zion tradition with which the author grew up, which has clearly been shattered and which cries out from the past, is answered from the Deuteronomic theology, also from the past. The Deuteronomic theology shows that Yahweh, who may have been at the centre of the Zion tradition, is in no way bound by it but is the sovereign Lord who punishes evil wherever it is found.

Albrektson's interpretation is nearer the mark than that of Gottwald, although the picture he paints may not do justice to the scene before him. Provan, while admitting that Deuteronomic and Zion traditions are clearly reflected in the book, questions Albrektson as to whether there is any resolution of the problems of the book within the book itself. Nevertheless, the student will find much that is helpful in Gottwald's chapters on the theology of Lamentations.

A quick skim through the five chapters of the book of Lamentations leaves the reader wondering whether we have here nothing more than a recital of the horrors and description of the subsequent misery of the people who have suffered the siege of Jerusalem, the terrible downfall of the city and of the entire state of Judah, with the final verse of the book simply adding to the negative atmosphere already created. But on a more careful reading of the book it becomes clear from certain passages that the faith of the poet has not been abandoned, that Yahweh is still his God. Indeed, one may reflect that the very existence of the book speaks of faith rising, Phoenix-like, from the ashes of disaster.

One cannot overemphasize the significance of the fall of Jerusalem in 586 BCE for the people of Judah. It was a watershed for their history and for their religion. The loss of statehood was in itself momentous, but with it came the loss of the Davidic line and the deportation of many of the important elements of the population. In addition, the destruction of the Temple meant the cessation of the cult and the sacrificial system. As Muilenberg puts it:

> When on the ninth of Ab the Babylonians entered the holy city, a new period was inaugurated in the history of biblical religion. The traditional faith had then to be read in the light of an event, catastrophic for Israel's political life and consequently supremely fateful for the quality of faith enshrined in the sacred history. Faith in a historical revelation was seriously threatened, and not a few came to conclusions of hopelessness that the facts of history seemed only too eloquently to warrant.

The effects of the entire episode of invasion and destruction were deep. Many in Judah who had been half-hearted in their loyalty to Yahweh would have adopted an 'I told you so' attitude. Yahweh was unable to keep his promise of protection; his very dwelling place was no more. Some may have considered Josiah's reforms to have been dangerous, and an offence to other deities, and that Judah was now paying the price. Some would have abandoned Yahwism altogether in favour of other cults, while others would have included Yahweh along with other deities, embracing a syncretistic religion. The view that Babylonian gods had shown greater strength than Yahweh must have been popular in some circles, while there appears to have been a resurgence of the practice of magic and astrology (cf. Fohrer). Some, the believers in the inviolability of Zion, will have been disillusioned, to put it mildly. The author of Lamentations belongs to

7. The Theology of the Book

yet another grouping, namely, those loyal to Yahweh. While great sadness pervades the book, and while the poet is evidently moved and sickened by the horrors of the situation, there is little sign of doubt displayed. This is a point worth pondering. The poet remains loyal to Yahweh. Nowhere do we find a tendency to syncretism; not a trace of a view that credited the fall of Jerusalem to the superior strength of the enemy or its gods. But as Gottwald says,

> that the prophetic response to the catastrophe was not inevitable may be seen in the attitude of those fleeing to Egypt who adopted the worship of the Queen of Heaven, inasmuch as for them Yahweh was defunct (Jer 44). Second Isaiah's vigorous polemic against idols implies that many Jews were entranced with the worship of Babylon (cf. Isa 48.5). And the descriptions of Ezek 8 and Isa 57 show that throughout the sixth century foreign cults penetrated Judah and won numerous adherents among the Jews.

There is ample evidence that the poet recognized the historic nature of the disaster. Throughout the five poems we find abundant reference to the downfall of Jerusalem and to the effect of that on the life of the people. Indeed, almost every verse rings out with words describing the awful severity of the situation. So extravagant is the language, and so repetitious, that one must conclude that the purpose was to emphasize the unique nature of the disaster. But the style merely assists, for the words themselves are sufficient and significantly powerful. The personified Jerusalem says to passers-by, 'Is there any sorrow like my sorrow?' (1.12; cf. 2.13). And this is further emphasized by the reference to Sodom in 4.6: 'the chastisement of the daughter of my people has been greater than the punishment of Sodom, which was overthrown in a moment, no hand being laid on it' (cf. Gen. 19). Throughout the Old Testament the destruction of Sodom (and Gomorrah) was regarded as the ultimate in divine judgment (cf. for instance Amos 4.11). But here the poet virtually says, 'We now have a new byword for disaster! Although Sodom's punishment was great, it was swift and sudden; in addition, Jerusalem's was long and drawn out. No hands were laid on Sodom, but hands were laid on Jerusalem!'

The fact that the Day of Yahweh concept is alluded to in Lamentations as if it were in the past and had referred to the fall of Jerusalem is a further indication that the author felt that Jerusalem had experienced the ultimate judgment. The emotional description of the fall of Jerusalem and its aftermath leads the poet (and the reader) to ask the question 'why?' Here we must imagine the hostile context I have sketched above: the sceptics, the apostates, the disillusioned as well as the loyal but subdued Yahwists. The poet's answer to the question 'why?' is in line with the Deuteronomistic theology with which he was familiar. This great punishment had taken place because of sin. It was Yahweh's response to the sin of the people. The poet conveys this, first, by confessing the sin of the people on a number of occasions (1.5, 8-9, 14, 18, 20, 22; 2.14; 3.39, 42; 4.6, 13, 22; 5.7, 16), and, secondly, by using a range of vocabulary to cover all aspects of sin: *peša'* ('rebellion'; 1.5, 14, 22; 3.42); *ḥēṭ'* ('miss, failure'; 1.8; 3.39; 4.13, 22; 5.7, 16); *'āwōn* ('crookedness, iniquity'; 2.14; 4.6, 13, 22; 5.7); *mārâ* ('be contentious'; 1.18, 20; 3.42). We should note that specific sins, such as idolatry or cruelty, are not mentioned (cf. Gottwald), although the poet occasionally spells out the guilty categories: population (1.5), prophets and priests (5.13) and forefathers (5.7). In mentioning the latter—'our fathers sinned, and are no more; and we bear their iniquities'—the author is probably mindful of Exod. 20.5, and more especially of the argument in 2 Kgs 21.8-15 which seems to lay the blame for the disaster on several generations of evildoers.

It is, therefore, quite clear from the text of the five poems that Israel's sin has led to this disaster. There may, however, have been those who would have accepted this argument but who would have attributed the disaster to other deities' being offended and angered by Josiah's reforms. The author of Lamentations is therefore at pains to make it absolutely clear that what has happened is not only because of sin but is the work of Yahweh (1.5, 12-15, 17-18, 22; 2.1-9, 17, 20, 22; 3.1-18, 37-39, 43-45; 4.11, 16; 5.19-20, 22). This is especially clear in 2.1-9 where Yahweh is depicted as an enemy warrior, ruthlessly laying waste the city and Temple, and slaughtering

7. *The Theology of the Book* 115

almost indiscriminately. In this sustained passage the poet makes certain that although many will say that the Babylonians were the enemy, that it was they who tore down the strongholds, wrecked the Temple, brought to an end the festival observance and rejected king and princes, one must not forget that the Babylonians were just a tool in Yahweh's hand. It is Yahweh who is the chief actor in this drama.

The author is also careful to note that Yahweh is not in a fit of irrational rage; his actions are a planned, if angry, response to the sin of the people. Hence his statements: 'the Lord is in the right' (1.18); 'in his wrath he has broken down the strongholds' (2.2); 'the Lord in his anger has set the daughter of Zion under a cloud' (2.1); 'the Lord determined to lay in ruins the wall of the daughter of Zion; he marked it off by the line' (2.8); 'the Lord has done what he purposed' (2.17); 'the Lord gave vent to his wrath' (4.11).

From what we have already observed, we may say that the author of the book of Lamentations felt that he and his people were at the end of an epoch but that the catastrophe of the fall of Jerusalem should have been expected, in that the people had sinned themselves out of Yahweh's favour. On top of this doom and gloom we have glimpses of the poet's (and the people's) despair, and the feeling that Yahweh has now cut off relations with Israel: 'The Lord has scorned his altar, disowned his sanctuary' (2.7); 'The Lord has done what he purposed' (2.17); 'though I call and cry for help he shuts out my prayer' (3.8); 'so I say, gone is my glory and my expectation from the Lord' (3.18); 'Thou hast wrapped thyself with a cloud so that no prayer can pass through. Thou hast made us offscourings and refuse among the peoples' (3.44-45); 'water closed over my head; I said, "I am lost"' (3.54); 'Our end has come' (4.18); 'hast thou utterly rejected us?' (5.22). One is reminded of the depths of alienation expressed by Job: 'Oh that my vexation were weighed, and all my calamity laid in the balances! For then it would be heavier than the sand of the sea' (Job 6.2-3; cf. 19.10).

And yet, all is not doom and gloom. One of the remarkable things about the Old Testament in general is that in the midst of adversity there is often a glimmer of hope. Sometimes it is subtle, as in the case of the Deuteronomistic history, which might have ended with the deportations after the fall of Jerusalem. The editor, however, added a final note describing the favourable treatment of the deported king, Jehoiachin, in Babylon (2 Kgs 25.27-30). This would have given hope to those in exile (where Kings was edited), and to those who remained in Palestine, that all was not yet lost. This is seen more clearly in the prophetic literature. Hosea strongly attacks the people of the Northern Kingdom for their apostasy. Yahweh says: 'I will be like a lion to Ephraim, and like a young lion to the house of Judah. I, even I, will rend and go away, I will carry off, and none shall rescue' (5.14); but this is followed by a prayer in 6.1-3 where hope in Yahweh is expressed. Again, Micah, who at 3.12 declared that Jerusalem would become a heap of ruins, declares at 5.2 a future hope for the people of Judah: 'But you, O Bethlehem Ephrathah, who are little to be among the clans of Judah, from you shall come forth for me one who is to be ruler in Israel'. And Isaiah, who paints a very gloomy picture at 9.4-5, also continues: 'For to us a child is born, to us a son is given; and the government will be upon his shoulder, and his name will be called "Wonderful Counsellor, Mighty God, Everlasting Father, Prince of Peace"' (9.6). The situation is similar in Job. I have already alluded to his despair in ch. 6; but in ch. 19 there breaks forth hope which the reader hardly believes possible: 'Oh that my words were written! Oh that they were inscribed in a book!... For I know that my redeemer lives, and at last he will stand upon the earth' (19.23-25).

We might expect to find hope in the book of Psalms. After all, it did serve as a prayer book for ancient Israel, and as such contains many songs of praise. But it is not so logical to find hope shining through gloom and despair in poems such as the psalms of lament, individual and communal; and here we are clearly reminded of Lamentations. Psalm 73, whose writer is in turmoil because the wicked appear to prosper and thrive, eventually moves into a passage which affords relief from the despair, and where we see great hope expressed in God.

In the light of the general tenor of Old Testament literature

7. The Theology of the Book 117

we might say that it would be out of keeping *not* to find hope expressed in some form in Lamentations. (Ecclesiastes is, perhaps, an exception, but here too the editorial passage 12.8-14 ensures that the last word is a positive one.) The author of Lamentations gives us a hint that he has not given up all hope, in that he has, in the first place, composed this literature. If all hope in Yahweh had gone there would have been little point in penning these words, and in such an artistic fashion. If the fall of Jerusalem is the end, why try to ponder its significance, its meaning? If Zion-theology has failed, why not draw a line under it all? If Yahweh has become like an enemy, why not link up with another, say a Babylonian, deity? The very fact that he puts pen to paper is an indication that the author's faith is still intact.

It is remarkable how the author of Lamentations, although reduced at times to expressions of extreme gloom and despair (2.11; 3.7-8; 5.22) is able to declare that Yahweh has acted fairly (1.18); that, although complaining that prayer is unheard (3.44), he calls Israel to pray to Yahweh (2.18-19), and offers appropriate words for that purpose (2.20-22). But the most important material in this connection is that which proclaims confidence in Yahweh. At 3.21-23 the poet states that, against all the odds, he has hope, because he calls to mind that 'the steadfast love of the Lord never ceases, his mercies never come to an end; they are new every morning; great is thy faithfulness'. He continues in this positive vein in vv. 25-36. Again, a prayer in vv. 55-66 derives from that confession of trust; and there is confidence expressed in 4.22 that an end of the punishment is in sight. Chapter 5 is itself a prayer offered to Yahweh in faith and confidence that he is still in control: 'But thou, O Lord, dost reign for ever; thy throne endures to all generations' (5.19).

It is sometimes said that in the pre-exilic period the people of Yahweh were *henotheistic* (believing in one god without denying the existence of other gods), not *monotheistic* (believing that there is only one god), and that even in Deutero-Isaiah monotheism is only in embryonic form. This may be so; but in the book of Lamentations we are surely in the presence of someone who is an active monotheist. As mentioned above, there is no trace whatever of a belief that the catastrophe could have been caused by anyone other than Yahweh. How easy it would have been, in a polytheistic society, to have considered the possibility that other powers had been at work in the fall of Jerusalem! The only other protagonists in the allusions to the disaster are the enemies, but they are carefully described as being Yahweh's instrument of punishment: 'The Lord has commanded against Jacob that his neighbours should be his foes' (1.17); 'He has delivered into the hand of the enemy the walls of her palaces' (2.7); 'He has made the enemy rejoice over you and exalted the might of your foes' (2.17). It is important to observe that those who search the Old Testament for hints of a belief in the existence of other gods will find nothing to detain them in these poems.

What are we to make of the cry for vengeance in these chapters? At the end of ch. 1 the city prays that her enemies may suffer the fate that she has experienced: 'Bring thou the day thou hast announced, and let them be as I am. Let all their evil doing come before thee; and deal with them as thou hast dealt with me because of all my transgressions; for my groans are many and my heart is faint' (1.21b-22). Again, at the end of ch. 3, we have: 'Thou wilt requite them, O Lord, according to the work of their hands. Thou wilt give them dullness of heart; thy curse will be on them' (3.64-65). At the end of ch. 4 the poet taunts Edom, an old enemy, with the words: 'Rejoice and be glad, O daughter of Edom, dweller in the land of Uz; but to you also the cup shall pass; you shall become drunk and strip yourself bare... Your iniquity, O daughter of Edom, he will punish, he will uncover your sins' (4.21-22). Are not these sentiments unworthy of the mind we discern elsewhere in the poems? How may they be interpreted? The same phenomenon may be observed in the book of Psalms (for instance in Pss. 58, 69, 83, 149). Perhaps the most extended passage is Ps. 109.6-20, where the supplicant calls for a variety of misfortunes to afflict his wicked enemy. In Jeremiah 46–51, too, we find similar invectives against foreign nations.

In trying to understand these passages we must first keep in mind that the authors belonged to an era and a society

7. The Theology of the Book

which differed from our own in many respects. The author never really questions the justice of Yahweh's punishment on his people; furthermore, he understands that the enemies of Israel are in the hand of Yahweh and are his instruments in the destruction of Jerusalem and Judah. But the author does not hide his anger and his desire for vengeance with regard to these enemies; and if they are enemies of Yahweh's people they are enemies of Yahweh too! They deserve to be punished (cf. Ps. 79, where the poet appears to explain to God that *his* property has been attacked). Some scholars (for instance Gottwald) try to excuse these vengeful thoughts by arguing that they were prompted by the fact that the enemies had gone beyond Yahweh's wish: not content with conquering Judah, they had done so ruthlessly and with hatred for Yahweh's people. What we have here, it is suggested, is righteous indignation at atrocities. There is no doubt that the author is concerned that his people do not suffer more than they deserve. He will have believed that evil must be punished; and, since he lived at a time when there was no real belief in life after death, he will have expected that punishment would take place in this life. But these factors must all be seen in the context of Yahweh's universal rule. Yahweh is the judge of all the earth, and any wickedness will be punished—in Israel, yes, but also in other nations. The element of vengeance, however, bursts through the doctrine of Yahweh as supreme judge and remains an ugly, if understandable, feature.

Further Reading

Ackroyd, *Exile and Restoration*, chapter 3.
Albrektson, *Studies in the Text and Theology of the Book of Lamentations*, chapter 3.
G. Fohrer, *The History of Israelite Religion* (London: SCM Press, 1972).
Gottwald, *Studies in the Book of Lamentations*, chapters 3-5.
Kraus, *Klagelieder*.
W. McKane, *Tracts for the Times* (London: Lutterworth; New York: Abingdon Press, 1965), pp. 50-60.
M.S. Moore, 'Human Suffering in Lamentations', *RB* 90 (1983), pp. 534-55.

J. Muilenburg, 'The History of the Religion of Israel', *IB*, I (1956), pp. 292-348, esp. 330-35.

Provan, *Lamentations*, pp. 20-25.

Re'emi, *God's People in Crisis: A Commentary on the Book of Amos: A Commentary on the Book of Lamentations*, pp. 73-134.

Rudolph, *Das Buch Ruth—Das Hohe Lied—Die Klagelieder*.

R.B. Salters, 'Scepticism in the Old Testament', *OTE* 2.3 (1989), pp. 96-105.

Westermann, 'Lamentations', pp. 316-18.

—*Die Klagelieder*.

INDEXES

INDEX OF BIBLICAL REFERENCES

Genesis		19.4	20	6.7-8	104
1	20	20.1	37	9	91
10.11	19			10	91
19	113	*2 Kings*		18.5	31
24.3	24	14.23-25	21, 23, 55	18.7	31
24.7	24	14.25	20, 25, 47	25	87
37.21	37	14.27	45	30.4	31
		20	31	31.7	31
Exodus		21.8-15	114	31.20	31
1.15-21	56	23.28-30	79	31.23	31
20.5	114	24.1	80	34	87, 91
20.10	20	24.7	80	34.1	85
34.6	19, 22,	25	81	34.16-17	88
	26, 47	25.1	81	42.5	31
		25.4-5	97	42.8b	31
Numbers		25.12	98	46.5	110
22.22-35	44	25.27-30	116	48	110
				51	76
Deuteronomy		*2 Chronicles*		58	118
9.18	29	14.5	37	69	118
18.21-22	60	24.27	47	73	76, 116
28	110, 111	35.20-26	79	74	101
28.64-65	107, 111	35.25	95	76	110
		36.13-14	80	79	76, 101,
Joshua		36.16-19	70		102, 119
1-11	42	36.23	24	83	118
				86.15	26
1 Samuel		*Ezra*		89	101
15.10	48	1.2	24	103.8	19
		1.5	24	109.6-20	118
2 Samuel		2.4	24	119	87, 91
1.17-27	86	2.20	24	120.1	31
1.25-27	102	3.7	19	136.23	24
1.26	103			142.4	31
3.33-34	102	*Nehemiah*		143.4	31
12.13-15	57	9.17	26	149	118
1 Kings		*Job*		*Proverbs*	
9.23	37	6.2-3	115	14.5	85
17-19	20	19.10	115		
17.2	48	19.23-25	116	*Ecclesiastes*	
18.3-5	22			1.3	24
19.4-8	46	*Psalms*		12.8-14	117
19.4-5	25	2.6	85		

Song of Songs
1.7	24
1.9-11	86

Isaiah
1.10-12	86
9.4-5	116
9.6	116
23.1	19
38.10-20	31
40.9-11	86
48.5	113

Jeremiah
1.8	25
1.11	25
2.8	96
2.18	96
2.36	96
5.31	96
6.25	96
7	110
7.1-20	78
7.20	20
7.26	78
8.18-22	95
9	95
9.1	96
9.18	96
9.20-21	102
13.17	96
14–15	96
14	95
14.13-14	96
14.17	96
15	95
18.1	19
18.7-8	20, 60
18.8	47
18.11	58
20.7	95
23.11	96
25.5	58
26	96, 110
26.3	25, 58
26.15	25
27.12	80
29.10-14	58
36	58
37	58
37.5-10	96
37.12	37
38.6-8	95
38.28	97
40.11	82
44	113
46-51	118
52.28-30	81
52.30	82

Lamentations
1–4	86, 97
1	87, 89, 97, 99, 102, 106
1.1-11a	73, 102, 103
1.1-5	71, 72, 89
1.3	77, 99, 106, 107, 111
1.5	96, 106, 107, 110, 114
1.6a	86
1.8-9	114
1.8	90, 110, 114
1.8a	86
1.9c	102
1.11b-22	73
1.11c	102
1.12-22	103
1.12-15	114
1.12	72, 113
1.14	114
1.16	96
1.17-18	114
1.17	102, 118
1.18	90, 110, 114, 115, 117
1.20	91, 114
1.21b-22	118
1.22	91, 114
2	87-89, 97, 102-104
2.1-9	73, 103, 114
2.1	115
2.2	115
2.5	77
2.6	77
2.7	115, 118
2.8	115
2.10-17	73
2.10	103
2.11	96, 117
2.12	77
2.13-17	103
2.13	103, 113
2.14	96, 114
2.17	103, 114, 115, 118
2.17c	86
2.18-19	73, 117
2.20-22	74, 117
2.20	114
2.22	96, 114
3	87-89, 97, 104
3.1-18	74, 114
3.7-8	117
3.8	115
3.14	95
3.18	115
3.19-24	74
3.21-23	117
3.25-36	117
3.25-39	74
3.30	72
3.37-39	114
3.39	114
3.40-47	104, 105
3.40-42	74
3.42	91, 114
3.43-51	74
3.43-45	114
3.44-45	115
3.44	117
3.48-66	104
3.48-49	96
3.52-66	74
3.54	115
3.53-56	95
3.55-66	117
3.64-65	118
4	87-89, 97, 102, 104, 106
4.1-11	74
4.1a	86
4.6	91, 113, 114
4.8b	86
4.11	114, 115
4.12-16	74
4.12	77, 78, 110
4.13	91, 96, 98, 114
4.16	87, 114
4.17-20	104
4.17	74, 77, 87, 96

Index of Biblical References

Ref	Pages	Ref	Pages	Ref	Pages	Ref	Pages
4.18-20	74	Jonah		3.7-9	20, 30		
4.18	115	1.1–2.3	38	3.7	24		
4.19-20	97, 98	1.1-3	17	3.9-10	33		
4.20	71, 77, 95	1.1	21, 22, 45, 52	3.9	26		
4.21-22	74, 77, 118	1.2	20	3.10–4.3	34		
4.21	104	1.3	24, 33	3.10	18, 30, 34, 56		
4.22	104, 114, 117	1.4-16	17	3.11	34		
		1.4-6	17	4.1-5	18		
5	87, 97, 101, 117	1.5-6	24	4.1-4	38		
		1.5	24, 33	4.2-3	33		
5.1-18	75	1.5b	36	4.2	19, 22, 24, 26, 33, 55		
5.6	77	1.6	24				
5.7	91, 114	1.7-12	17				
5.13	114	1.7	24, 29	4.2b	59, 60		
5.16	91, 114	1.8	29	4.3	20		
5.18	77	1.9	20, 24	4.4	20, 30, 36		
5.19-22	75	1.10b	36	4.5	29, 34-37, 39		
5.19-20	114	1.12	24				
5.19	117	1.13-16	17	4.5a	36		
5.22	114, 115, 117	1.14	33, 52	4.5b	37		
		1.16	33	4.6-11	18, 30		
		1.17–2.1	17	4.6-10	38, 39		
Ezekiel		1.17	17	4.6	20, 38		
17.12-14	80	2.1	29, 36	4.7-9	38		
18.1-3	58	2.2-9	18	4.8	24, 34		
27.8-9	24, 25	2.2	34, 36	4.9	20		
27.25-27	20	2.3-10	20, 30	4.10	24, 38		
27.27-29	24	2.3a	31				
29.1-16	81	2.4b	31	Micah			
30.20-26	81	2.5	33	3.12	116		
31.1-18	81	2.5a	31	5.2	116		
34.6	25	2.6a	31				
		2.7	31	Nahum			
Hosea		2.8	34	1.2-3a	22		
1.2	19	2.8a	31	1.3	19		
5.14	116	2.9	32				
6.1-3	116	2.9a	31	Zechariah			
		2.10	18, 31, 36	7.3-5	71		
Joel		3	29				
1.13	25	3.1-5	18	Ecclesiasticus			
1.20	20	3.2-3	20	49.10	21		
2.13-14	25, 26	3.2	24				
2.13	19, 47	3.3	29	Matthew			
4.1-12	55	3.4	29, 35, 36, 39	12.40	15, 53		
				12.41	52		
Amos		3.5-10	38				
4.11	113	3.5	29, 30, 35	Luke			
5.2	102	3.6-9	18	10.30-37	59		
7.15	19	3.6	34, 36	11.29-32	15		

INDEX OF AUTHORS

Aalders, G.C. 49
Ackerman, J.S. 50
Ackroyd, P.R. 44, 49, 119
Aharoni, Y. 82
Albrektson, B. 66, 107, 110-11, 119
Alexander, T.D. 41-43, 48, 49
Allen, A.C. 13, 26, 39, 46, 48, 49
Anderson, A.A. 76, 82, 91
Andres, S. 16
Andrew, M.E. 48, 50

Bach, J.S. 68, 72
Baculard d'Arnaud, F.-T. de 68
Barr, J. 72
Barton, J. 69, 72
Baumgartner, W. 101
Begrich, J. 107
Berkeley, L. 16
Bernstein, L. 68
Bewer, J.A. 13, 29, 39, 42, 46, 49
Blayney, B. 93, 99
Böhme, W. 38, 39
Bright, J. 82
Brockington, L.H. 13, 49
Brunet, G. 99
Budde, K. 49, 86, 91
Burrows, M. 44, 50
Byrd, W. 68

Calvin, J. 53, 94
Camus, A. 16
Cannon, W.W. 99
Clements, R.E. 57, 58, 61
Cohn, G.H. 16
Coverdale, M. 94

Davidson, R. 65, 105
Daube, D. 61
Day, J. 32, 39, 48, 55, 61
De Wette, W.M.L. 30, 39, 91
Driver, S.R. 95, 99

Eissfeldt, O. 44, 46, 49, 72, 84, 91, 102, 105-107
Emmerson, G.I. 56, 61

Feuillet, A. 44, 50, 55, 61
Fohrer, G. 61, 112, 119
Freedman, D.N. 91
Fries, S.A. 99
Fretheim, T.E. 43, 50, 61
Frost, S.B. 82
Fuerst, W.J. 65, 82

Gadd, C.J. 106, 107
Garr, W.R. 91
Gaster, T.H. 107
Gevaryahu, H. 61
Goitein, S.D.F. 39, 61
Golka, F.W. 13, 14, 26, 61
Gordis, R. 65
Gottwald, N.K. 66, 70, 72, 89-91, 101, 103, 107, 109, 111, 113, 114, 119
Glück, J.J. 26
Gray, G.B. 92, 50
Gunkel, H. 45, 50, 101, 107
Gwaltney, W.C. 107

Handel, G.F. 72
Hardt, H. von der 93
Herbert, A.P. 16
Herbert, A.S. 65
Herrmann, S. 82
Hillers, D.R. 65, 69, 71, 72, 85, 91-93, 98, 105, 107, 108
Hitzig, F. 55, 61
Housman, L. 16
Huxley, A. 16

Ibn Ezra 34

Jahnow, H. 101, 108
Jeremias, A. 92

Jerome 68, 72
Johnson, A.R. 49
Josephus 31, 72

Kaiser, O. 50
Kaufmann, Y. 56, 57, 61
Keller, C.-A. 50
Kidner, F.W. 39
Kimchi 34, 52
Knight, G.A.F. 49
Knox, R.A. 87, 92
Kochanowski, J. 68
Kraeling, E.G. 29, 38, 39
Kramer, S.N. 106, 108
Kraus, H.-J. 66, 93, 108, 119

Lachs, S.T. 97, 99
Landes, G.M. 34, 39, 50
Lohfink, N. 35, 39
Löhr, M. 92, 99, 104
Luther, M. 42, 53, 88, 94

McDaniel, T.F. 106-108
McKane, W. 119
Magonet, J. 13, 33-35, 39
Malamat, A. 79, 81, 83
Marcus, R. 88, 92
Martin, A.D. 49
Meek, T.J. 65, 93, 99, 104
Moore, M.S. 119
Muilenburg, J. 112, 119
Munch, P.A. 89, 92

Nägelsbach, C.W.E. 65, 99
Nielsen, E. 49, 61
Noth, M. 83

Oded, B. 83

Payne, D.F. 61
Pfeiffer, R.H. 72, 88, 92
Philo 31, 44
Porteous, N.W. 105, 108
Provan, I.W. 65, 72, 83, 111, 119
Pusey, E.B. 41, 48

Quevedo, F. de 68

Rad, G. von 41, 48, 50
Re'emi, S.P. 65, 119
Ricciotti, G. 99
Robinson, D.W.B. 49
Rowley, H.H. 44, 54, 62
Rudolph, W. 14, 62, 66, 77, 99, 104, 106, 119
Russell, D.S. 95, 100

Salters, R.B. 110, 119
Sasson, J.M. 13, 22, 40, 48, 62
Saydon, P.P. 37, 39
Schneider, D.A. 22
Selms, A. van 27
Shea, W.H. 92
Smart, J.D. 13, 39, 49
Smith, G.A. 49
Soggin, J.A. 83
Stade, B. 105
Stravinsky, I. 68
Streane, A.W. 65, 93, 100

Tallis, T. 68, 72
Tigay, J.H. 68, 72, 106
Trépanier, B. 49
Trible, P.L. 13, 33, 40, 49
Tyndale, W. 31, 40

Viadana, L. da 68

Wade, G.W. 13, 40
Walton, J. 49
Watson, W.G.E. 85, 92
Watts, J.D.W. 14, 49
Weiser, A. 14
Wiesmann, H. 100
Wiseman, D.J. 80, 83
Westermann, C. 66, 108, 119
Wilson, R.D. 27
Wolfenson, L.B. 69, 72
Wolff, H.W. 14, 16, 27, 29, 33, 40, 46, 48, 50, 62
Wright, A.G. 49
Woude, A.S. van der 35, 37, 39, 40

www.ingramcontent.com/pod-product-compliance
Lightning Source LLC
Chambersburg PA
CBHW070336230426
43663CB00011B/2338